Between Species/ Between Spaces

Introduction

Peter McMahon
Founding Director,
Cape Cod Modern House Trust

The Cape Cod Modern House Trust (CCMHT) was founded in 2007 to collect, archive, and share documentation of the Outer Cape's important modern architecture, restore a group of endangered experimental houses owned by the National Park Service (NPS), and to relaunch them as platforms for new creative work.

The three derelict modern houses we have leased and restored now host our artist/scholar residencies, which seek to re-populate these dynamic structures with creative people, whose work relates to nature, the history of modernism, and the creative community that thrived here in the mid-20th century. Since its inception our project has been a close collaboration with the NPS and specifically the Cape Cod National Seashore, which acts as the steward of the houses, and their pristine natural environs.

In the past CCMHT has hosted designers, artists, composers, filmmakers, and writers. For this residency, curators Dylan Gauthier and Kendra Sullivan selected artists whose work overlapped in some way with the scientific research undertaken by NPS staff as well as by a wide range of visiting field scientists working within the Park's boundaries.

Wellfleet's modern houses served as laboratories, for their original inhabitants who sought empirical data to inform new approaches to visual art, curation, and the design of furniture, housing and urban spaces. Of particular interest is the informal think tank that was centered at the pond-side retreat of architect and academic Serge Chermayeff. By the mid 1940s, Chermayeff and his friends Bernard Rudofsky and György Kepes (along with their families, friends and students) were spending summers in Wellfleet — growing their beards, talking, arguing, and sitting by bonfires on the beach, and gathering research to support their own counter-cultural strain of modernism.

Chermayeff painstakingly diagramed possible relationships between housing and its urban context in hopes of providing users with the amenities of modern living while protecting them from the noise and disruption of thoughtless development. These proposals culminated in his seminal book *Community and Privacy.*

Living nearby in a cabin with no indoor plumbing, architect and writer Bernard Rudofsky took an ethnographic deep dive into pre-industrial cultures (especially Japan's) to rediscover and reclaim more human-friendly ways to eat, dress, build, and live. These inquiries resulted in a series of critical shows at the Museum of Modern Art and a series of pivotal books including *Architecture without Architects,* which championed ingenious and environmentally responsive, vernacular building traditions from around the world.

Artist and photographic pioneer György Kepes, who lived and worked nearby in a house designed by his life-long friend Marcel Breuer, founded the groundbreaking Center for Advanced Visual Studies at MIT with a mission of bridging the boundaries between art, science and design.

Today, the CCMHT is delighted to welcome a new generation of creators to become inspired by these house/laboratories, ensconced, as they are, in the landscapes that inspired their design.

— Wellfleet, May 2018

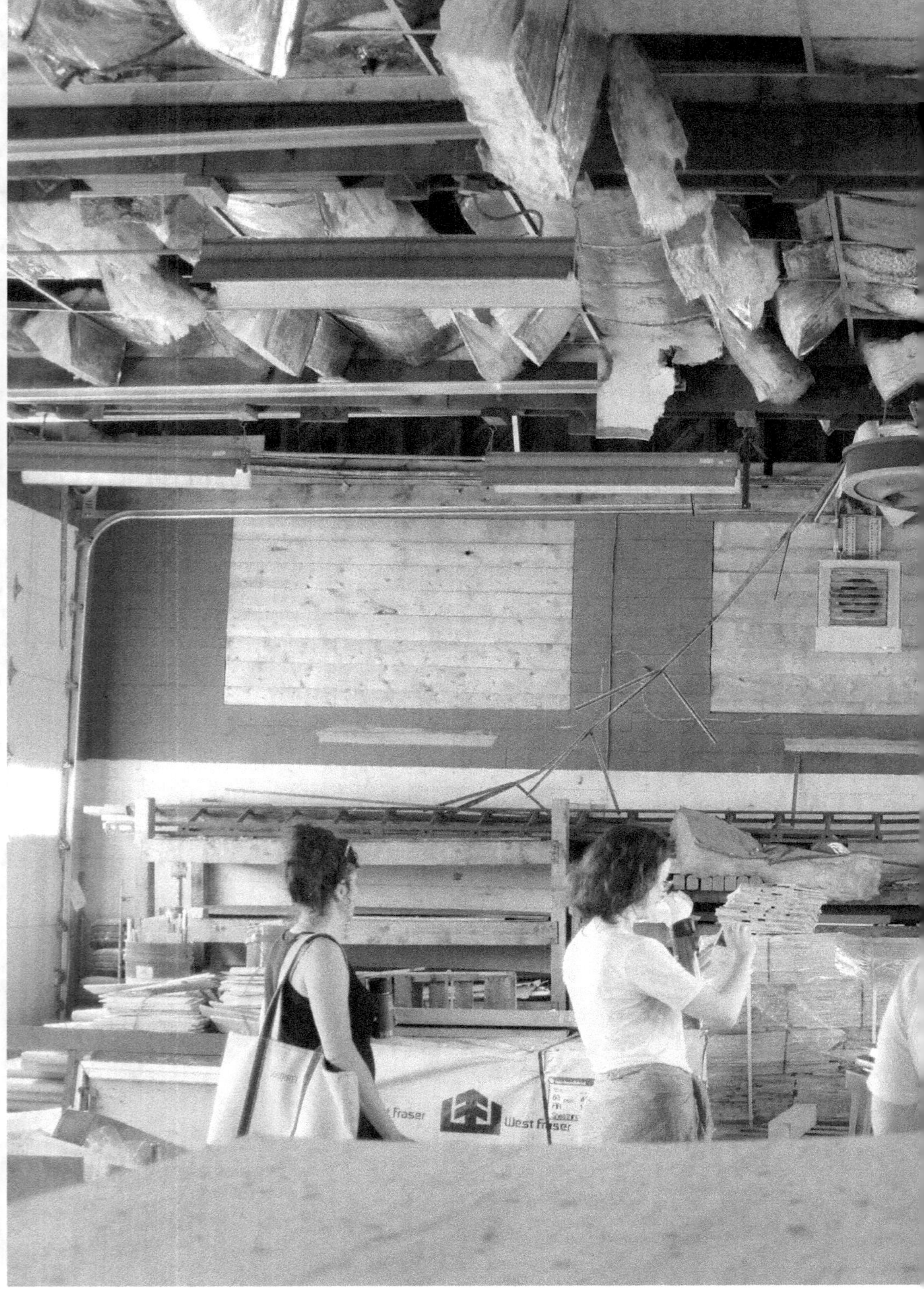
West Fraser

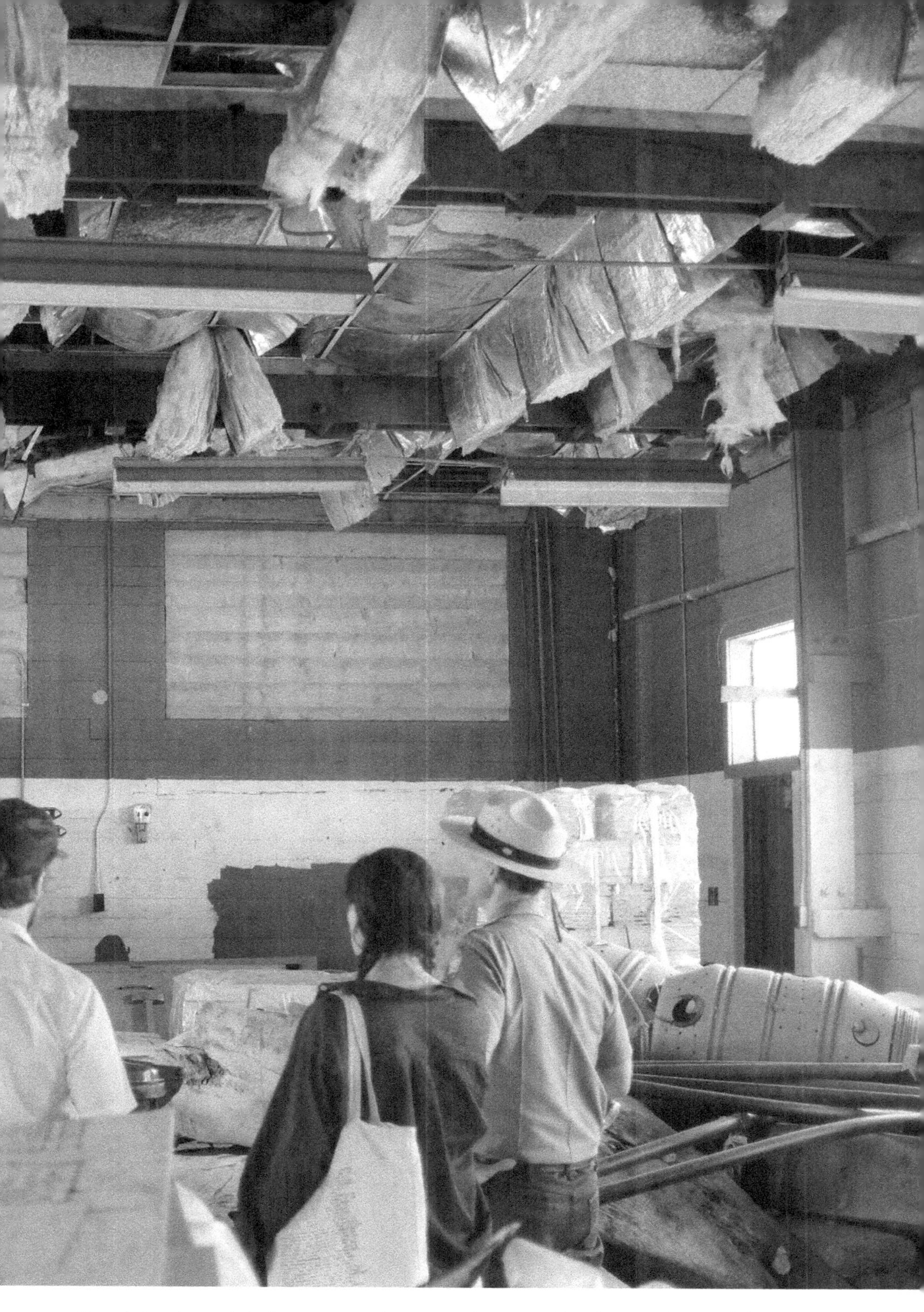

Resident artists are given a tour of the NPS archives
accompanied by curator Bill Burke.

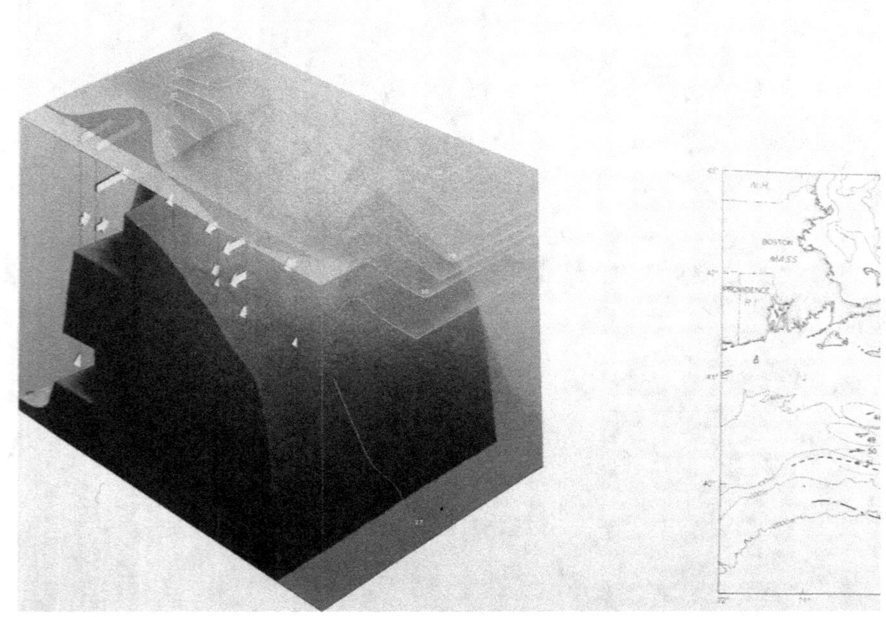

Between Spaces

Kendra Sullivan and Dylan Gauthier
Curators and Co—Directors,
The Institute for Ocean Art and
Science

> "Wishing to get a better view than I had yet had of the ocean, which, we are told, covers more than two thirds of the globe, but of which a man who lives a few miles inland may never see any trace, more than of another world."
> — Henry David Thoreau, *Cape Cod*

When Thoreau walked from Eastham to Province-town in 1849, he followed a path along a coastline that has long since vanished. Is it fair to say then that the Cape Cod that Thoreau knew no longer exists? As we pored over photographs from the early 1900s in the National Park Service office in Truro, MA one afternoon, we remarked that much we saw was familiar but so much had changed. The area we had come to know as the piney forest of Wellfleet appeared in photos as barren stretches of dune, the result of the deforestation that occurred within the first forty years of European settlement. The forest had been regrown over the intervening century. Similarly, areas of beach had been washed out only to be rebuilt again. Then there were the dramatic scenes of entire villages being hauled back from the edge of dunes. It is commonplace to refer to the Cape as a place of continual change. Indeed, three feet of the Cape's sandy coast is swept out to sea each year on average, and in some places, as much as eight feet of the coastline can be lost. Yet these very regular conditions of change are themselves now subject to new, previously unanticipated alterations, as anthropogenic climate change ushered in a new and unprecedented era of sea level rise, strange weather patterns, unexplained bird and marine mammal death, and disease vectors that threatened humans and non-humans, and an entire way of life. Encountering the site as artistic researchers, we were intrigued by the question that haunts many artists struggling to come to terms with climate change: how can we depict or create a reliable study of a place that is undergoing near constant transition?

In November of 2016, we were invited by Peter McMahon to take part in a research residency at the Cape Cod Modern Houses in Wellfleet, on a theme of art and science collaboration. It is not known to most casual tourists to the Cape that in any given year, over three-dozen independent research projects are being run by the National Park Service station inside the National Seashore. These projects bring researchers to stay on the Cape from all over the US and abroad. Some of the projects have long durations, envisioned and carried out over decades, dependent on grants and government funding. This was, in fact, the main subject of our conversation during our first meeting with Peter, over dinner at the Wicked Oyster in Wellfleet. It was Thanksgiving weekend, and little else was open in that corner of the Outer Cape. The darkness of Wellfleet in the off-season was intensified by an existential sentiment of darkness encroaching on us after the 2016 election, and the dis-ease echoed in our talk that night, and in the deep red glasses of wine we shared in the quiet bar.

Earlier, we'd spent the day tailing a group of students and staff from Harvard's Department of Visual and Environmental Studies program, as Peter invited us along for a speed tour through CCMHT's three restored properties and the Kohlberg house, a small a-frame that Peter hoped to take a lease on later that year. Our conversation turned from politics to climate change to art to architecture to conservation and to the future of the National Seashore under a new federal regime whose hostility to science and the arts in equal measure gave us pause. It felt like a good time to grow alliances between the arts and sciences.

We stayed the night at Weidlinger House, and awoke to a startling light reflecting off the pond, along with wild turkeys in the driveway, a tailless raccoon trapped in a garbage bin under the house who needed rescuing, and a quiet morning lulled by the sound of the winter waves pummeling nearby Cahoon Hollow Beach. Wellfleet in the off season had already, almost instantly, become one of our favorite places in the world. We enthusiastically planned a return in January to meet Mark Adams, the NPS cartographer and sedimentary geologist who is also a painter and a poet, and who would become our spirit guide to navigating an art and science collaboration with the NPS. Mark handed us a thumb drive which included a PDF of the book he illustrated and co-authored with Graham Giese and Jeffress Williams for the US Geological Survey: *Coastal Landforms and Processes at the Cape Cod National Seashore, Massachusetts*. This, along with Peter's *Cape Cod Modern: Midcentury Architecture and Community on the Outer Cape*, were our trusted field guides to the place.

On the drive back to Brooklyn, the idea for our project expanded from a single performance or exhibition into something that would allow us a longer duration in which to work. Peter was incredibly supportive of this idea, as he was of extending the invitation to Jean Barberis, Josh Edwards, Marie Lorenz, Katherine McLeod, Nancy Nowacek, Jeff Williams, Lynn Xu, and Marina Zurkow. Following in the spirit of interdisciplinary collaboration of CCMHT's Bauhaus expats, each artist would be invited to pair with a researcher at the NPS and to construct a new research project.

At the start of the residency in early May, we shared Weidlinger House, Kugel/Gips, and Hatch, basking in family-style meals at night and sunset cocktails at on the ample porches. We opened the doors of these houses to researchers and scientists we would meet through the NPS including whale spotters and rescu-

---

[1] We are writing this during a government shutdown, on the day the EPA has supposedly run out of money, the NEA surely not far behind. Online we see signs posted on the doors of temporarily closed NPS visitors centers around the country. This is the third shutdown in the same number of years. The "nonessential" services provided by scientists or artists are put on hold. Any time sensitive projects will no doubt face setbacks and delays. Art and science. The act of communicating in concentric circles. The reverberations between the known world and the unknown and intuited world.

ers, naturalists, biologists, geologists, and other researchers from the National Seashore. We passed the
days hiking and writing and painting and recording
sounds and digging in the dirt. We soon met Sophia
Fox and her intrepid interns, Bill Burke, the NPS
curator and archivist, and Stormy Mayo and Laura
Ludwig at the Center for Coastal Studies (CCS). We
visited the NPS archives and found documents of the
ongoing quest to understand some truth of this place
in the form of bound records of studies and theories
of change. We met Gwen and her husband, the wave
counters who for 15 years had been measuring the
angle and attack of waves offshore the Truro NPS
station in a refashioning of the historic coastal survey
by Henry Marinden, and to study the effect of climate
change-related sea level rise on coastal erosion. In
the research projects we encountered at the NPS,
we witnessed a spirit of exploration and inquiry, a
messiness in process, peppered with a serious enjoy-
ment of nature that being in a place as breathtakingly
beautiful as the Outer Cape can not help but pro-
duce.

This same spirit of inquiry and serious fun that seems
at the heart of the NPS research station can be found
in the artwork produced by our collaborator-residents
over four separate visits from early 2017 through the
spring of 2018. During these stays, the artists and scientists shared ideas and dinners, walked the beaches
and wooded trails, exchanged tools and method-
ologies, and learned about each other's work. The
exchange culminated in an exhibition at Kugel/Gips
house in Wellfleet, and a public talk at the Salt Pond

Visitor Center in Eastham in May, 2018.

For the residency, Marina Zurkow spent time in dialogue with Stormy Mayo and devised the series of right whale banners that were exhibited on the front of Kugel/Gips house in Wellfleet and now hang in the offices of the CCS. Zurkow's banners pay tribute to a few of the recently lost whales and memorialize a species in decline. Marie Lorenz shadowed the work of NPS researcher Sophia Fox, who is leading the multi-year study of the restoration of the Herring River that once flowed through Wellfleet Harbor and Truro. The ongoing Herring River Restoration Project is the largest tidal restoration project in New England, and covers over 1,000 acres of degraded estuarine habitat. Jeff Williams composed a series of drawings that trace the way one of the modern houses, Weidlinger House, captures and casts light on the surrounding regenerated forests. They are a sketch of the incremental change we take for granted as the Earth moves around the Sun. Mark Adams's paintings and diaristic writing explores the role of observation and audience in scientific and artistic creation. His mylar paintings are in conversation with his life-long research on coastal ecologies and reveal a host of hidden relationships between creatures. Nancy Nowacek discovered a link between the chemical composition of microplastic particles, their behavior in nature, and tongue twisters ("She sells PVC shells..."). Joining advocacy to art production, in an ensuing performance Nowacek invites us to adopt ocean plastics (as "PETs") by organizing community beach cleanups. Jean Barberis led us on a culinary journey of regional delicacies and wild-foraged dinners, one of which is reproduced herein. Lynn Xu authored a series of poems and a slideshow on oceanographic themes, drawing on her time staying at the Hatch House. Joshua Edwards took a series of walks that would have followed in Thoreau's footsteps if the shoreline had not been so radically altered in between the two poets' peregrinations. Our own work, taking a final form of a video and sound recordings, formed in conversation with Laura Ludwig, Mark Adams and Bill Burke of the NPS, and poet and naturalist Elizabeth Bradfield, and delved into the aesthetics of the presentation of science knowledge, drawing on the NPS archive as source material.

This book presents a record of the residency and the exhibition, but more broadly we hope it reveals the closeness of the artistic and scientific processes, as ways of seeing and ways of exploring this site of great change and great wonder that is the Outer Cape.

— New York, December 2018

The curators acknowledge that the lands that this residency and exhibition are being held on are the original homelands of the Mashpee Wampanoag, Aquinnah Wampanoag, Nipmuc, and Massachusett tribal nations. They acknowledge the painful history of genocide and forced removal from this territory, and honor and respect the many diverse Indigenous peoples still connected to this land on which they have been invited to assemble this group of artists and scientists. They pay respect to the Mashpee Wampanoag Tribe in particular, which is based on Cape Cod and has inhabited present-day Massachusetts and Eastern Rhode Island for more than 12,000 years.

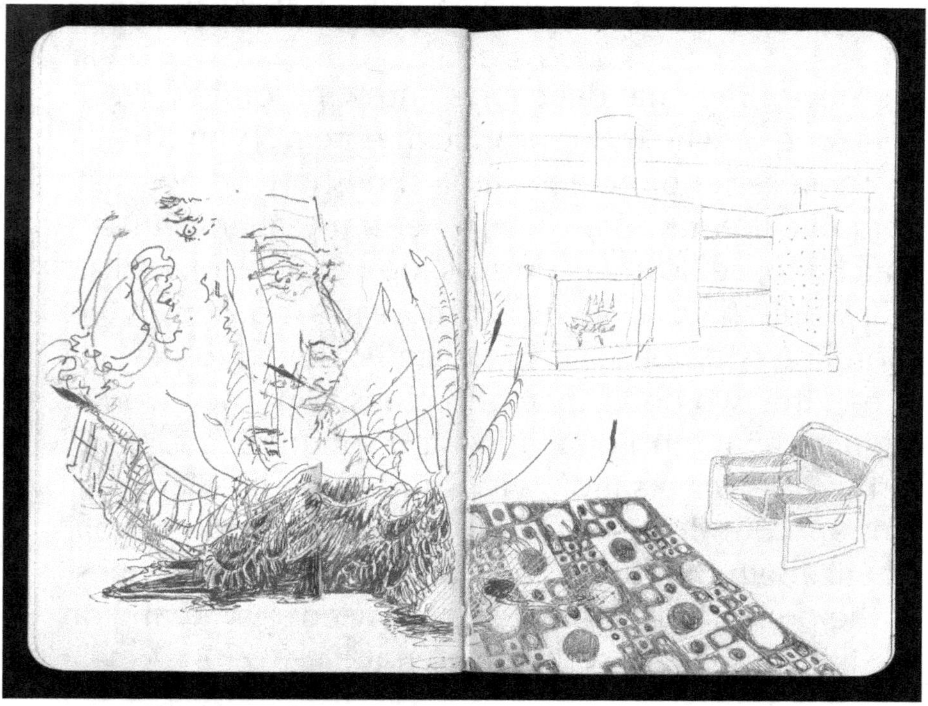

Marie Lorenz, *Sketches of Weidlinger House*, 2017

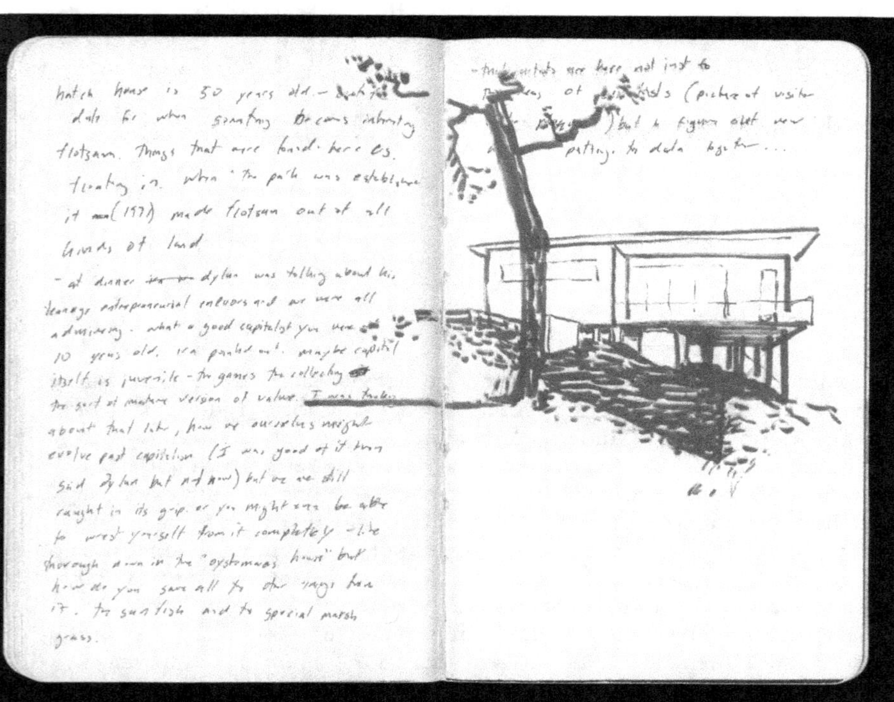

Diary from the Southern Corner of the Gulf of Maine, Small Sea Perched above the North Atlantic on the Continental Shelf

Mark Adams

2017.10.18 8:00 pm

Wednesday North Truro 62 degrees F, flat seas / gentle swell 20 degree angle from the right. The sea edge is blurry and fluid and biblically unreliable. We go to the beach when it's stormy, to see the ocean preach. We count waves to gage the forces that are carving Cape Cod into a new shape — as they have since the last glaciers, 10,000 years ago. Call it weathering; beaches are made of the sand taken from cliffs down drift, the leveling of everything.

Today the beach is abruptly scarped, 3-plus feet lopped off the berm and taken out to sea. If we estimate a right triangle 3 feet by 20 feet by 5 miles that's (60 times 2600 divided by 5 equals 31,200 cubic feet of sand in one tide. Enough to rebuild a half mile of dune, the entire Head of the Pamet.

This afternoon a run from South Pamet to the highest place on the cliff, a looping bluff top trail, sun raking tall grass. Thinking, making lists in my head that will disappear at the trailhead. Messages I need to send, loops to close, fires to ignite. There's a regular call for mapping skills on disasters: hurricanes, wildfires, floods. Disaster relief can be an escape from awkward social expectations with holidays looming.

For a moment I am recognized everywhere. I captured the high tideline by GPS on a 4-wheeler in the fading hours of daylight on Monday, trailering to Nauset Beach in Orleans alone, wondering if my tie-downs would hold. An official town pickup truck rolled up to ask what in the heck I was doing. He recognized me from 10 years ago when I made him a map of Pleasant Bay, which he used authoritatively for years in town meetings. He warned me about the fading light as I set off at a pace along the sand road to the inlet — zigging along, steep foreshores scooped in crescent hollows, engrossed in the manual shift, giving sidelongs at the chalky blue surf. (This particular color, glacial blue with purple undertones and white tips, patrolled by squads of horse-headed seals.) The primary dune diminishes from thirty down to three feet and the glowing western sky overcasts, slanting the shoreline. Around the south spit into the bay, its scattered shoals, amid questions from gulls, cormorants, and sanderlings. Spit to spit, inlet to inlet. And I'm back — driving directly up the trailer ramp, then twenty miles of highway and I am offloading the day into the dark lab.

This week, classes visited the museum show: exuberant 5th-graders and subdued 8th-graders. I jumped to their questions like a rabbit. Beautiful moments: a girl observed that there was a drawing-language for feelings. Now I write this and feel the air go out. I'm depleted.

Every night my roommate plays piano, flipping through sheet music like a parody, sour hint of whisky and the abrasive whiff of cigarette ash. Chords stretched like yoga, mixed with the fear of a coming heartache.

2017.10.20 10:45 pm

Clearest night, stars drilling holes in the thick cold blackness. I curl into my back, today's ache. A day of missed deadlines, how time gives you only one thing at a time.

Andrew is expansive, home from a late shift waitering: it's a profound moment for science, he says with unexpected gravity, a dark hour when it all might just tip. Endless night or the lifting dawn? Not sure if I can hold off this sundowner syndrome.

Outside there's an aluminum bucket with a dead weasel, perfect two-toned sleekness, little nose and distinguished grasping hands. Our wildlife biologist retired and today I cleaned out a freezer full of other meso-mammals, bats and birds and box turtles and some ziplocks I didn't dare to open. A few bait bags stuffed with chicken legs and chopped squid for the turtle traps. The animals had been accumulating in a freezer for 20 years, stacked otter, fox, fisher, a dozen box turtles, as many weasels, a few moles, a peregrine, a shearwater, a tern, songbirds, and bats. Many snakes and toads too bound up to unwrap. I buried the mess of it in a pit behind a shed, but stuffed some tupperware full of little creatures and a sharp-shinned hawk in my freezer. A peregrine waits in a box by the back gate. Emptying the freezer in homage, these are things I was meant to do. Each animal a precious universe, tiny articulations of finger bone and slicked pelt. Crows huddle in the giant maple with prying eyes. Everything I'm doing fascinates them.

Silence now. Some nights deserve an all-nighter. Diamond night, just a chill, no wind, one truck downshifting up the hill and silence. Andrew smokes outside the screen door, the butt glows, the kitchen hums or it's just my ears, cicadas, faintly.

Strangely, I am being nudged off my own cliff, the end of a chapter. The few people that piss me off are not going anywhere, so maybe I must. Last time I cut the cord, there was desperation and loneliness that didn't lack romance. It took two years, or three. Then twenty went by. There were the relationships, each a limited success. People died, not the ones you expect and I miss them but the wound that is really mortal is fear of the next loss, spin the bottle, whoever we can't afford to lose. Maybe everything, when the global cascade buries today's anguish, all the clocks stopped at once.

In a story, the character moves away from death, far away, and becomes unknown. Living death to his friends. That distance is filled with palpable pain, thick as this night sky. You want it, but can you bear it? In movies and books, I always skip ahead, I have to know. Skidding toward the inevitable you get flipped. You save the kid and then you have to babysit. Break it, own it. We know the trite thing is coming and we pant for it.

Thinking about the endings. We really have never been here before — as we watch the oceans boil or dry up. So much to let go of. But then look, some last shiny thing revives us and we are hypnotized with our luck. On we go, living hungrily, kicking aside the debris.

Earlier on a cliff above the edge of the Gulf of
Maine, I waved my arms over the ocean, speaking
to a young cameraman about scale, orders of
magnitude: 100 feet down to the surf line, 50 miles
out to the shipping channel and a 150 miles south,
the continental abyss, 12,000 feet down a seafloor
canyon. Today the sea is gently whipped, a wrinkled
sheet pulled over the basins and rounded forms, the
underneath asleep.

2017.10.23 Monday 9:30 pm

Another run, the beach sucking up the last warmth
of October. Veering off down Firehouse Road to the
roadkill barn. It was like a sacrifice, and a bonding
ritual. The deft hand with the small sickle-shaped
flenser. Carport light, folding table, and the muscular
hands cradling furry animals, perfectly formed and
full of wonder. One otter drowned in a turtle trap,
another a road kill. We are the vulture tribe, says
young S. His wife is there, barefoot with a glass of
wine and a long fur collared coat. S's father, sure and
silent with the flenser. A girl with one long skinny
braid called Peaches and a silent boy, Eric.

The lush fur is peeled back, breast and arms, up the
jaw and down the legs, carefully dodging the musk
glands, revealing a gentle disarmed meat puppet, not
unlike a generous pork loin. Grimace of canines and
floppiness until the skin is laid out like a little hoodie.
There are jokes and fascination and I'm chilled by the
sweat from my run as the night mist rises around. We
are all in awe, and taking each step with deliberation
and drinks. Finally the old man splits the ribcage

and we lean in to see the plum-shaped heart, the tiny stomach whose unlucky contents we care not to examine. I massage the fisher's pliant paw, so small and gentle, still fleshy and particular. I'm telling them about the feast of the sacrifice, Islam's second favorite holiday where the whole family unwraps a slaughtered ram, savoring it in stages, encircled in kinship. Whatever reminds us we are animals and makes us soft and pliant and human, in utter awe at the mysterious, transparent life force that spills out.

These days between summer and the dark months feel like a reprieve before the plunge into the dark, a few hours bracketed by nightfall and dawn. Walking back from the sacrifice, phone dead, no moon, near pitch dark, feeling for gravel and wheel ruts, finally breaking into a run as I reached pavement, following the centerline. The houses lit within, all strange, night embracing. Finally the chill got me and now I shiver in the kitchen, coat and running shorts and a pot of late night coffee, looking for a spark.

```
2017.10.28 10:00 am Saturday.
62 degrees and sunny.
```

The autumnal sun gages its angle to the kitchen window. Now it rakes across my eyes between 6:59 and 7:01, finding a way between the treetops and eves, scattering light, gilding the morning, and making it difficult to read anything.

Things wake me in the night, tomorrow's meeting, the slight I perceived. Why am I awake? It's mostly an excitement and impatience. Let's do this thing. The last dead animals have been sitting in a box in

the rain, not quite smelling but slowly draining their
spirit, a drop of blood pooling out of an eye socket.
But the falcon is impeccable and shows no sign of
decline. I hang it by it's perfect recurved talons and
it assumes a bent pose as if craning to see a blur of
songbird motion.

2017.10.29 Sunday evening.

Rain rolls in making the fall chill count double.
We've kept the illusion of warmth till now but there
is a moment that flips the seasons, like ponds turning
over the deep water mixing with the shallow until it's
cold and rich all the way to the bottom.

Yesterday's trail run was melancholy and excellent,
almost quenching the doubting voices, hammering
them into the sand with each step. Another chance
to walk out onto the map and dive into an imaginary
world. The day was not lost — retreat to the studio to
make animal portraits for day of the dead. Rapidly,
a drawing emerges for an *ofrenda* altar — for the
animals. A peregrine and a fisher, bones and shells
and feathers drawn on a sheet of birch veneer.

2017.11.02 20:30 Thursday.

Lyme disease again, an excuse to feel like this: achy
and confused and manic. Feels like a badge and
I'm a dope for letting myself get bit. I wonder what
these repeated infections are doing to my brain
and nervous system. But it hasn't really slowed me
down. Picture myself on bearberry hill watching
the wind comb the reeds along the river below. As

if this were a wild place and I was a good animal,
I'd drift into a mindless flow, watching. If something
stirred in the grass — some ungulate upwind — my
attention would wake almost involuntarily. We are
fools for pattern and rhythm — but we are electrified
by the interruption. How else would we stalk a
deer? Making drawings, making experiences, we
could appeal to our animal nature and make a prey-
surprise. Every gallery visit would be an invitation
to stalk, an engagement of the unthinking brain
suddenly confronted by a puzzle, a delight, a trick to
elicit a metaphoric honeypot at the end of it all.

2017.11.29 Wednesday evening.

I've unloaded the contents of my carefully
constructed environment into stacks of chaos. The
load-out from the museum to the these rooms at
Quail Meadow where I sit among boxes, shivering
and pouring more tea into my acid stomach. What
could be more boring than despair? Making is a state
of being that stops clocks. I can pour ink and wield
a brush, cover skin with letters, cyphers. It would
pass time but I want to stop time. Hide under stories.
Then trade the stories for brushed letters, pin striping,
the filigree on a Moroccan screen. Trade the stories
for 100 miles on a bike fighting cancer, a thousand
hours of blues scales on a cello. Paths carved down a
mountain of man-made snow, S-curves stopped with
parentheses of face-plant angels.

But from one ending, the making machine is primed.
For a pause I think only of this, the ice monkey
around which is stitched my skin and furs and lashes,

ready to collapse into a crisp pool. Sendak's Gollum.

2017.11.30 Thursday last morning of the month.

How did it go? Knocked a few of them off. Satellites, meetings, polygons, a cortado here, a few glasses of wine. Did a life drawing of a kid I know, a portrait in blue. He took a picture of it to save. In between jam jars of Côte du Rhône, we sniffed this giant bud of blueberry goo sativa. Heady with paranoia and indolence. Now we laugh about replacing the tar in our lungs with fluffy rainbow unicorn semen. Every sign gives me a lump. My solid ground has liquified. I am sheet flow. Laugh about it, see the irony, the hurt I've caused. The tide circles around and we get swamped.

2017.12.05 Tuesday

A day at a coastal conference in which I learn that the Greenland icecap has a gravitational pull on the ocean. When it melts, sea levels in the North Atlantic will fall. When the Antarctic ice sheet melts, seas in the North Atlantic will rise in compensation. But overnight, the Gulf Stream could grind to a halt and change everything.

2017.12.09 Saturday

A Summer Field Drawing Class

Wandering and getting lost in Truro, foraging for words and images. Lost and found, in plain sight, without a destination. Paths of the back shore, the evasive forest, maritime woodlands, pine barrens and thickets, dune walks in words and pictures. The observant hand, close vision, footsteps on dune paths. Scanning the horizon, we explore places you've probably never been in the hollows and dune fields with pen, pencil, and sketchbook, collecting impressions and generating pages. Materials:

9x12" sketchbook or larger
a selection of soft pencils 2B, 4B, 6B
ink pens, felt tips, fountain pens
medium sized bamboo brush
a bottle of ink (walnut or india black)
optional: water colors in a few tubes or a box
water bottle, paper cups
towel or blanket for sitting
walking shoes, hat, sunscreen, insect repellent

The Swerve of Robert Jay Lifton

How is this crisis like any other turning point in history, any other hinge of disaster? Robert Jay Lifton spent much of his career as a psychologist and social historian weighing the human meaning of nuclear weapons and related nightmares. Lifton is concerned at how these moral rationalizations damage us, creating skewed self-serving logic while the ultimate toxic contamination degrades the planet. Climate change, the greenhouse gas inversions that are cooking the earth's habitats and remixing its seas, are framed as another kind of toxic contamination. How will we fare as social beings, hive dwellers.

History proceeds between big accidents: the profound ripples triggered by terrorism, the electoral quirks that give us minority rule and erratic presidents. The next accident may be a plague of birds falling from the sky or some unmeasurable disappearance of insects, cascading into famines. Incongruously we'll be endlessly scrolling potential dates and cat videos while all of Amazon's digital shelves are bare of bread and milk. Our toxic menace is not just climate change, not just the collective unconscious shadow of a flooded planet. We are a hive that is ready to swarm, gather like a smoked cluster, torpid bees clinging to a trunk, awaiting a leader and a new hollow cavity.

Climate scientists doing the important work have refined their measurements of sea ice and icecap meltwater dynamics, drought cycles, and Gulf Stream salinities. We may know a lot about our tipping points just before the kettle whistles. Bio-geo-engineers dither impressively with salts and seeds for the clouds, with domes and industrial injectors to re-calibrate the Gaia machinery. Engineers might even invent cars that emit nothing but rainbows and dew. But our rapacious selves and our hungry corporations worry me. There's no victory lap. Geologists remind us: rocks and planets endure and lack the capacity to rue anything. Tsk tsk, say the mountains, they have their own work to do, million year vortexes of continental plates floating on the half-baked mantle.

A Roethke epigraph doesn't signify hope, rather an

endgame self-knowledge — "the eye begins to see" — the same clarity as the dawn firing squad.

As a kid, I rode along in the station wagon to buy corn and pumpkins from farms at the edge of town. As a returning college student, I rode along to shop the malls that replaced the farms. As an adult, we skirt the ghost-town malls to catch an airport shuttle in a box-store parking lot. The devastation is complete. My parents bought a tract house for my grandmother, bordering a ragged creek and fields of crows and foxes. Now you can see through the thin forest curtain along the creek to the newer tracts. My brother saw a fox there recently and called the police. Mine is the generation of environmental experiments — some barely called in by an environmental moment that gave us NEPA, Clean Air, Clean Water, and Wetlands, all in the space of an election cycle. Then there was Bopal, Nuclear Winter, and near extinction of whales.

Robert Jay Lifton describes the accumulation of malignant normality. He pins our hopes on a swerve, scenario when vivid knowledge spurs a cultural turning point, when received normality is overwhelmed by the daily evidence: sunny day high water, crumbling tundra, early leaf-out, the global unrest of migrant populations fleeing crop failure and inundation. Official proclamations replace scientific findings, web pages disappear but in spite of policies, the navy moves its berths, farmers change their crops, ticks flourish, ski resorts make snow. We adapt in our lives in spite of government headlines and outdated rules.

Hark back to an enlightenment moment when the world was ready for a new view of the material universe, atoms taking equal agency with angels. What does it take to swerve? Forsake the tribe for the reality of your own lying eyes.

2018.01.03

This time, we had almost no lead up. A burningly frigid Christmas week, Andrew's nose dead white with frostbite. The last hour before sunset, I ran out to see the breach, the high tide licking the scarp of dune shrubs. Surely the midnight tide would be just a precursor to tomorrow's overtaking storm surge.

Chunks of ice blown off the bay are scattered on the highway in Wellfleet. I keep thumping my indoor-outdoor thermometer and wonder what it's really measuring. Numbers seem nutty — Fahrenheit-Centigrade, positive-negative. Waiting for the cyclone bomb. The ocean sublimes with sea smoke. I report with fascination the wave run-up over the once steep dune, deep fans of sand over the back-barrier marsh. The sand whipped into bedforms swirling in several directions which the geologist called "supercritical," meaning the water can't flow fast enough to get out of its own way. At high tide the breach is all quicksand. I stumbled deep to the thighs in the slurry. It was a laugh, but then the wind, a fever howl, and my pants froze to my skin in an instant. There was nowhere to go, but the reporter found me and recorded a frenzied interview in the front seat of my Subaru, leaving sheets of freezing wet sand across the seats.

A year in couple of days. Always eager to see the end of things, but the geologic minute could take some patient decades. I had just enough light left to take stock of the bathhouse and what was left of the road. I imagined our forty-year plan being overtaken in under five. There's a ski cabin five hours from here, there's a dinner date by a wood stove an hour over the bridge. I gotta find a mechanic to fix my headlight, change my oil, fill out some hiring forms, get a dump sticker, skin some roadkill. Tomorrow we'll make coffee and check the wind. Snow won't overtake the rain until past noon. Then there'll be hurricane winds, record breaking pressure drop, and a hard freeze. But on we'll go. And it's only the third of January.

Works

Mark Adams
Jean Barberis
Joshua Edwards
Marie Lorenz
Nancy Nowacek
**Kendra Sullivan
& Dylan Gauthier**
Jeff Williams
Lynn Xu
Marina Zurkow

Mark Adams

Mark Adams

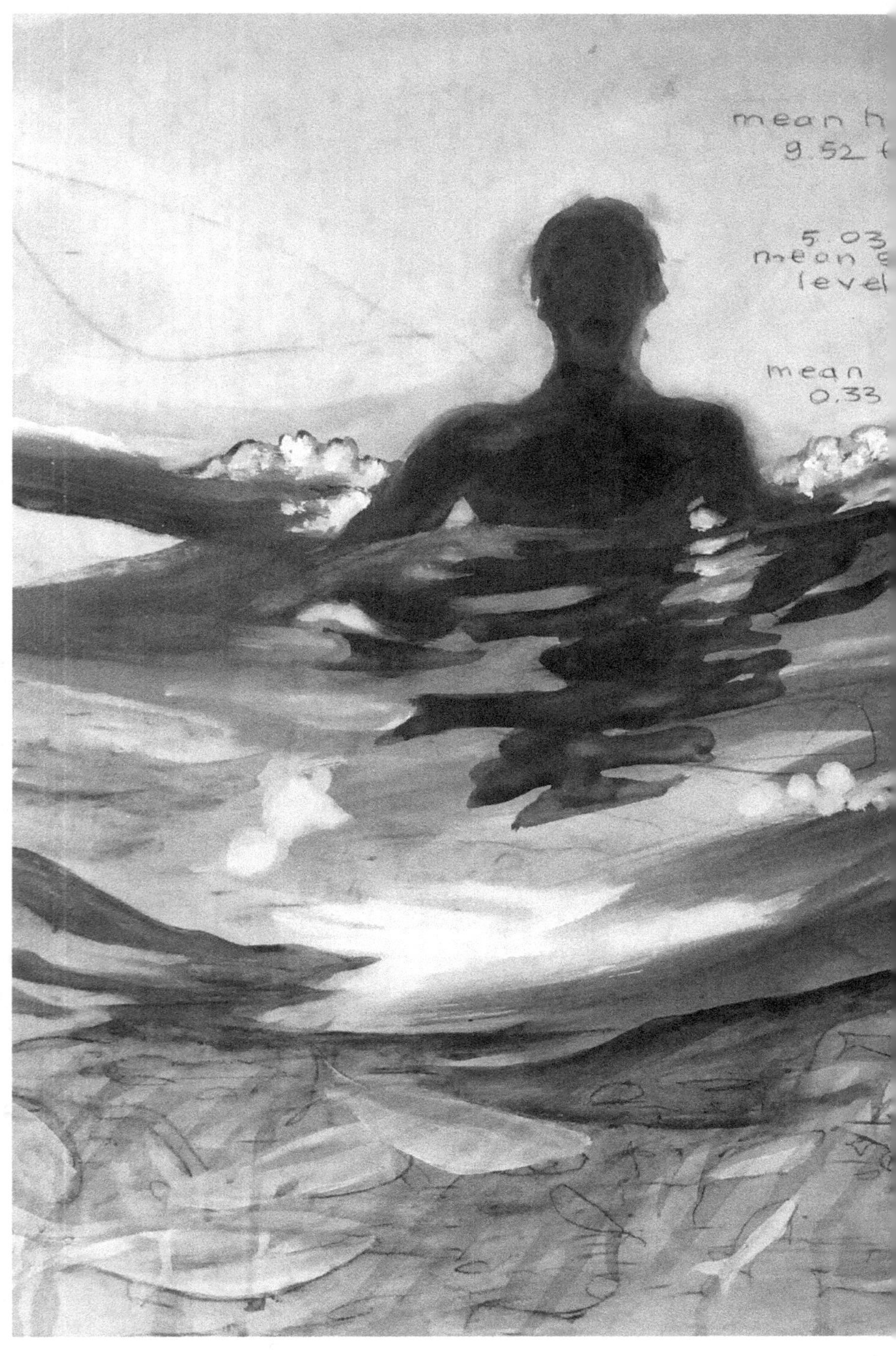

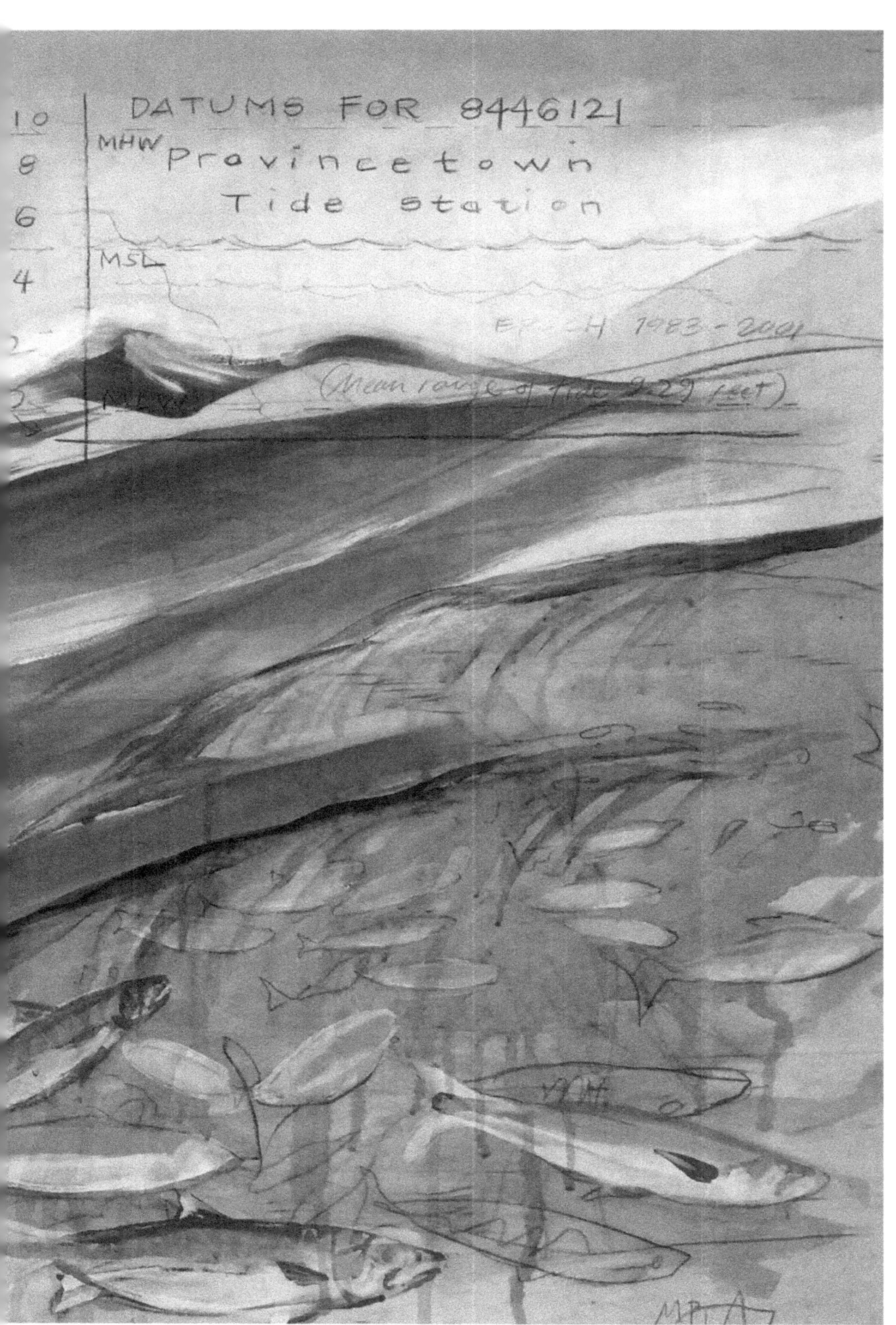

Provincetown tide station, mackerel, oil
pencil on wood, 2018

Mark Adams

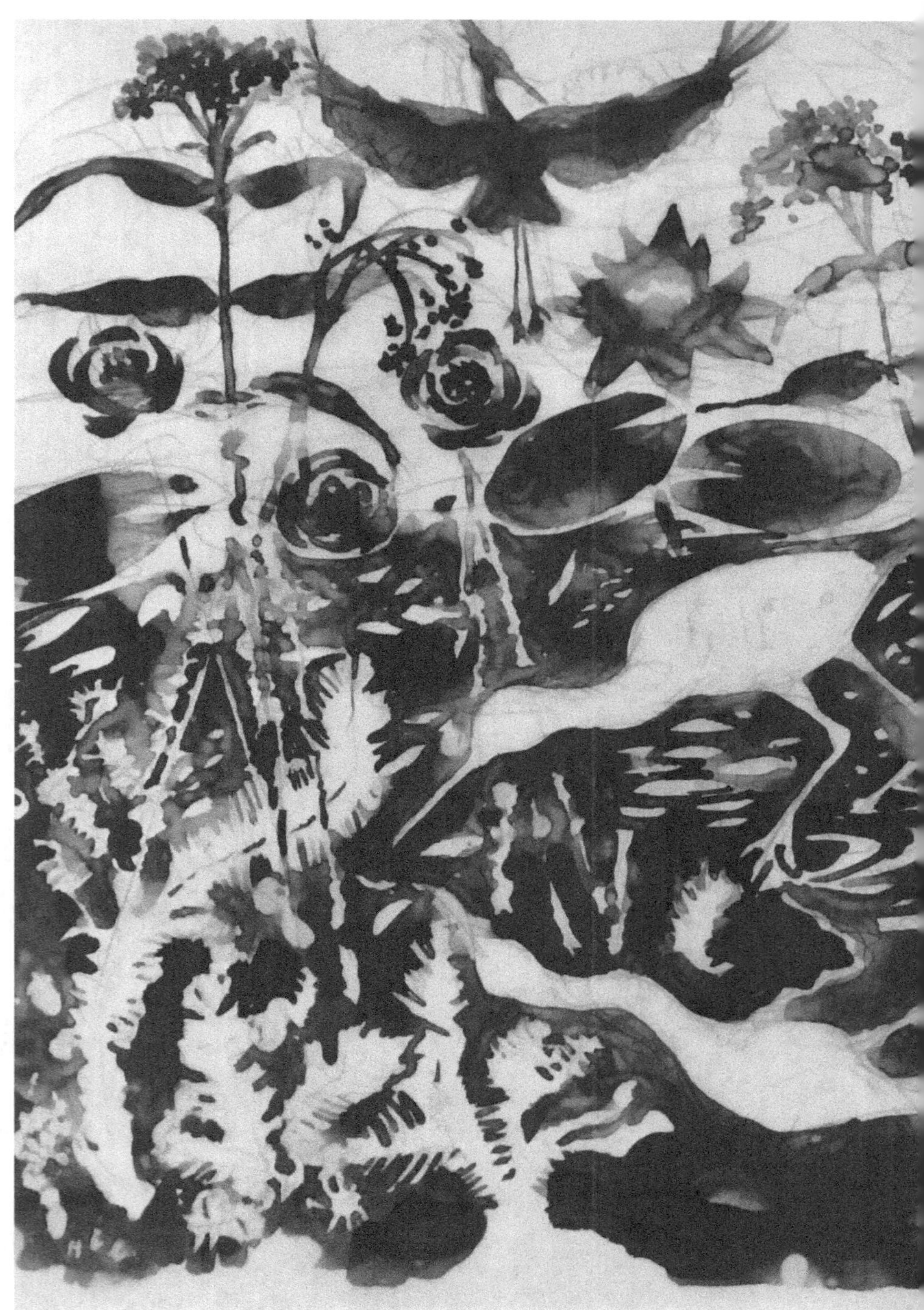

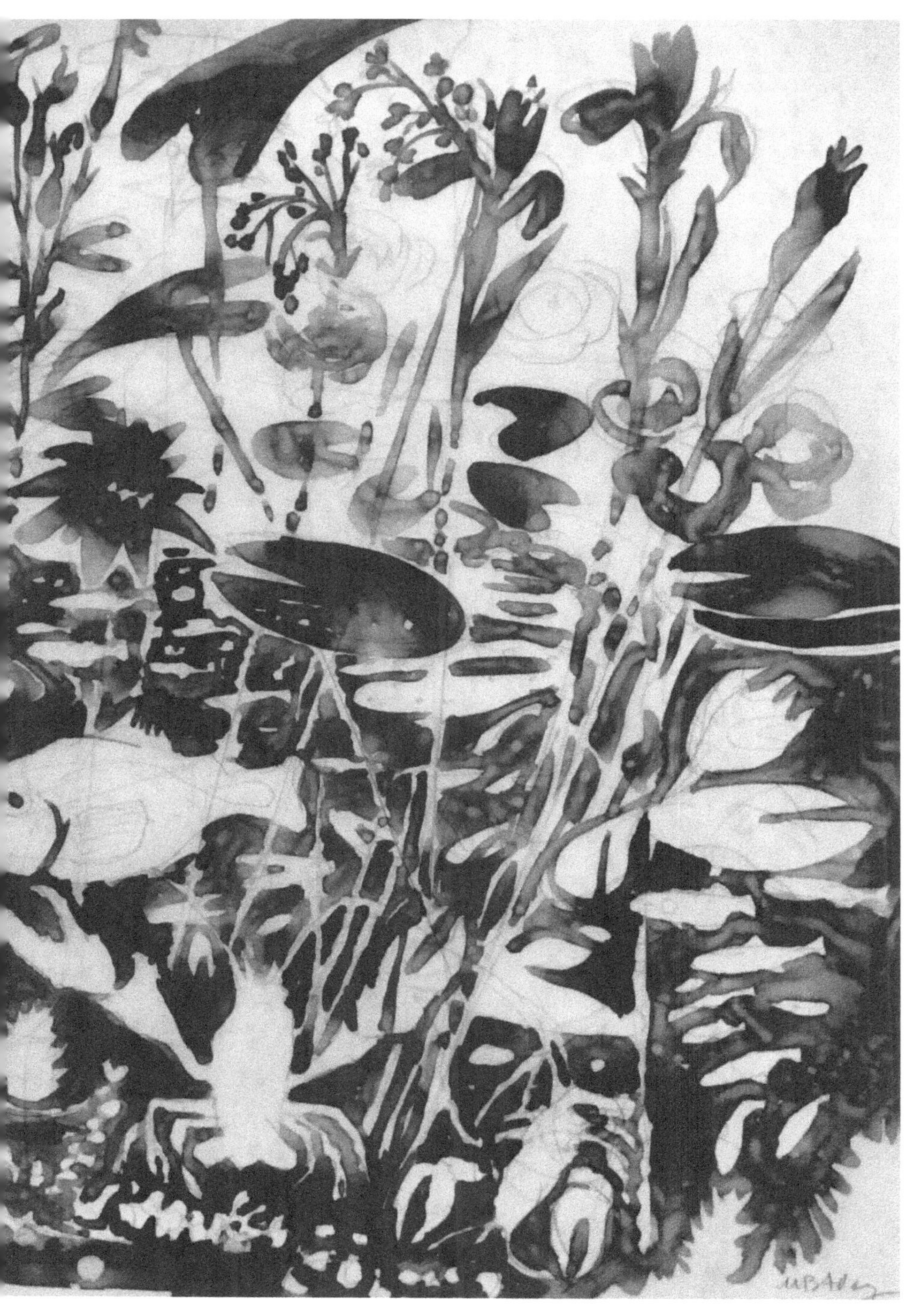

Salt marsh, red ink on mylar, 2018

Mark Adams

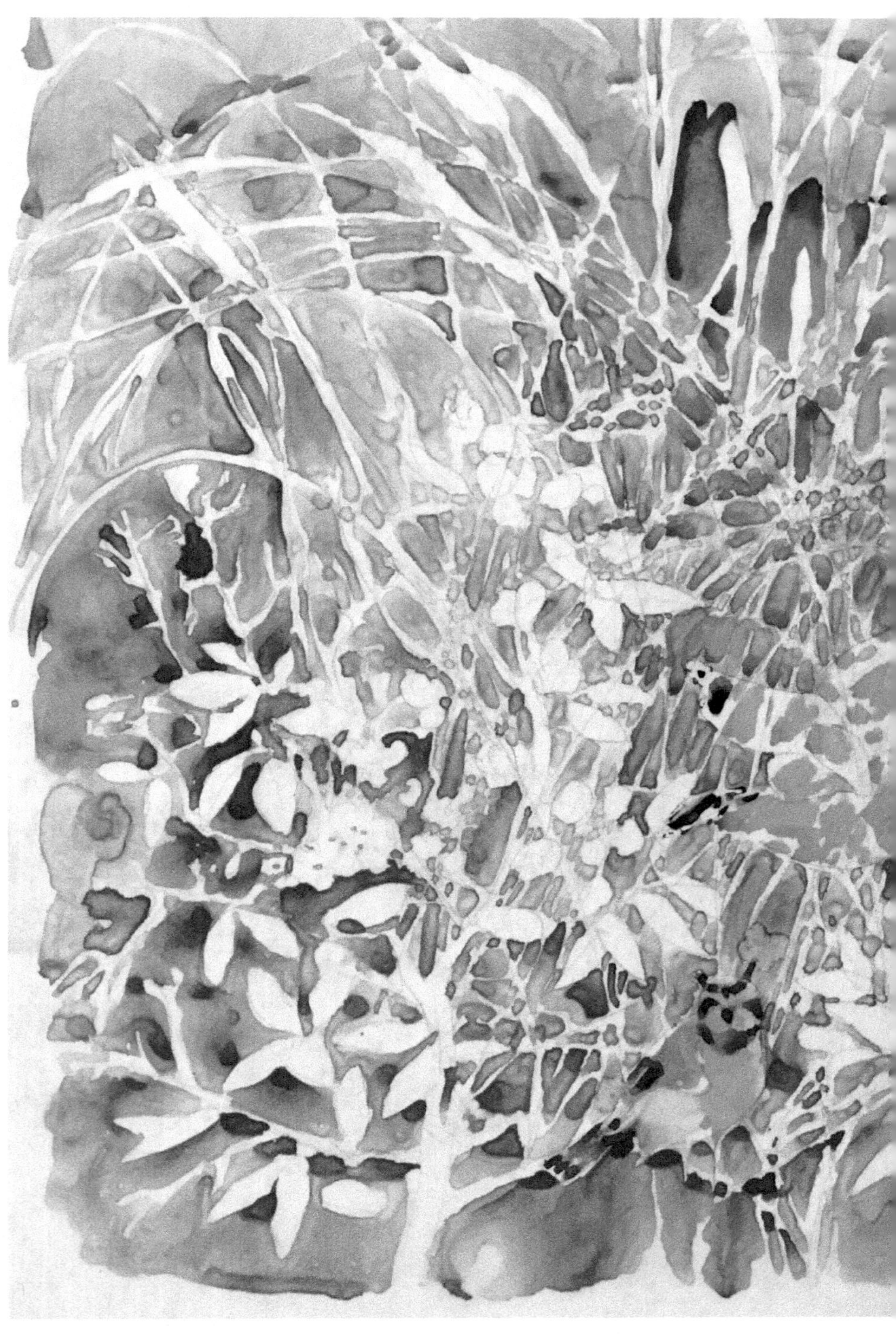

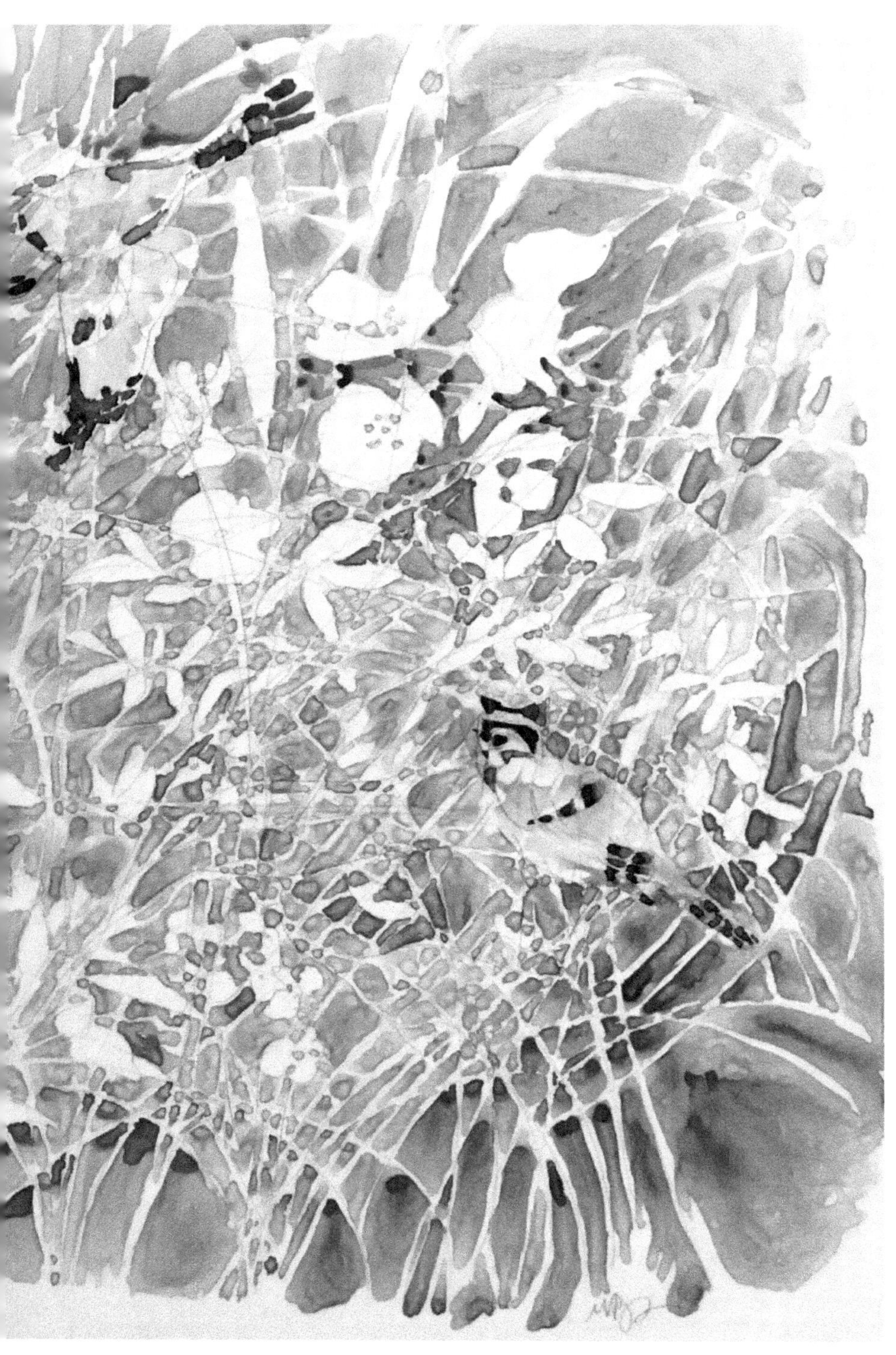

Horned larks, beach grass yellow/black ink on mylar, 2018

Jean
Barberis

A Recipe for Crab à la JoJo Which Can Be Adapted for Any Seafood (For 4 People)

```
6 medium potatoes
8 tomatoes
2 large crabs
1 onion
1 head of garlic
1/2 cup white wine
1 jalapeño or piment d'espelette
1 pinch of saffron
1 egg yolk
olive oil
butter
```

1. Oil and salt your cast-iron pan.

2. Preheat oven to 400°.

3. Cut the potatoes in 1/4-inch slices, lay face down in the pan with the jalapeño (cut in half lengthwise) and the garlic (whole garlic cloves, unpeeled) Bake till the potatoes are done (about 30 minutes).

4. In a saucepan, sauté onions and combine peeled, chopped tomatoes, bring to a boil, then let them to simmer in a saucepan with a little bit of water until you have yourself a nice tomato sauce.

5. Cook the crab in boiling water or bouillon for 5 minutes, cut and pick the flesh. Save the guts and carcass to make a bouillon, add onions, garlic, and

herbs.

6. Once the potatoes garlic and jalapeño are done, set them aside.

7. Peel the garlic cloves and chop the half jalapeño finely (you can substitute *piment d'espelette*). Grind to a creamy paste in a mortar. Add the egg yolk, a pinch of saffron, and salt and keep grinding till the mixture emulsifies. Add olive oil until the you obtain a roasted garlic aioli.

8. Filter the bouillon, and whisk a cup of it into the aioli, along with a spoonful of flour and white wine. The result should be a creamy white sauce. Add your tomato sauce to the mix.

9. In your pan or a baking tray, layer the potatoes, crabs, and sauce. add freshly chopped parsley. Bake for 10 minutes.

10. Serve with a crisp white wine like *Picpoul de Pinet*.

Crab à la JoJo was prepared by Jean Barberis at Kugel/Gips House as part of a dinner with Mark Adams, Marina Zurkow, Nancy Nowacek, Peter McMahon, Kendra Sullivan, Anthony Lee, Keith Vincent, Dylan Gauthier, and Katherine McLeod.

Joshua Edwards

Joshua Edwards

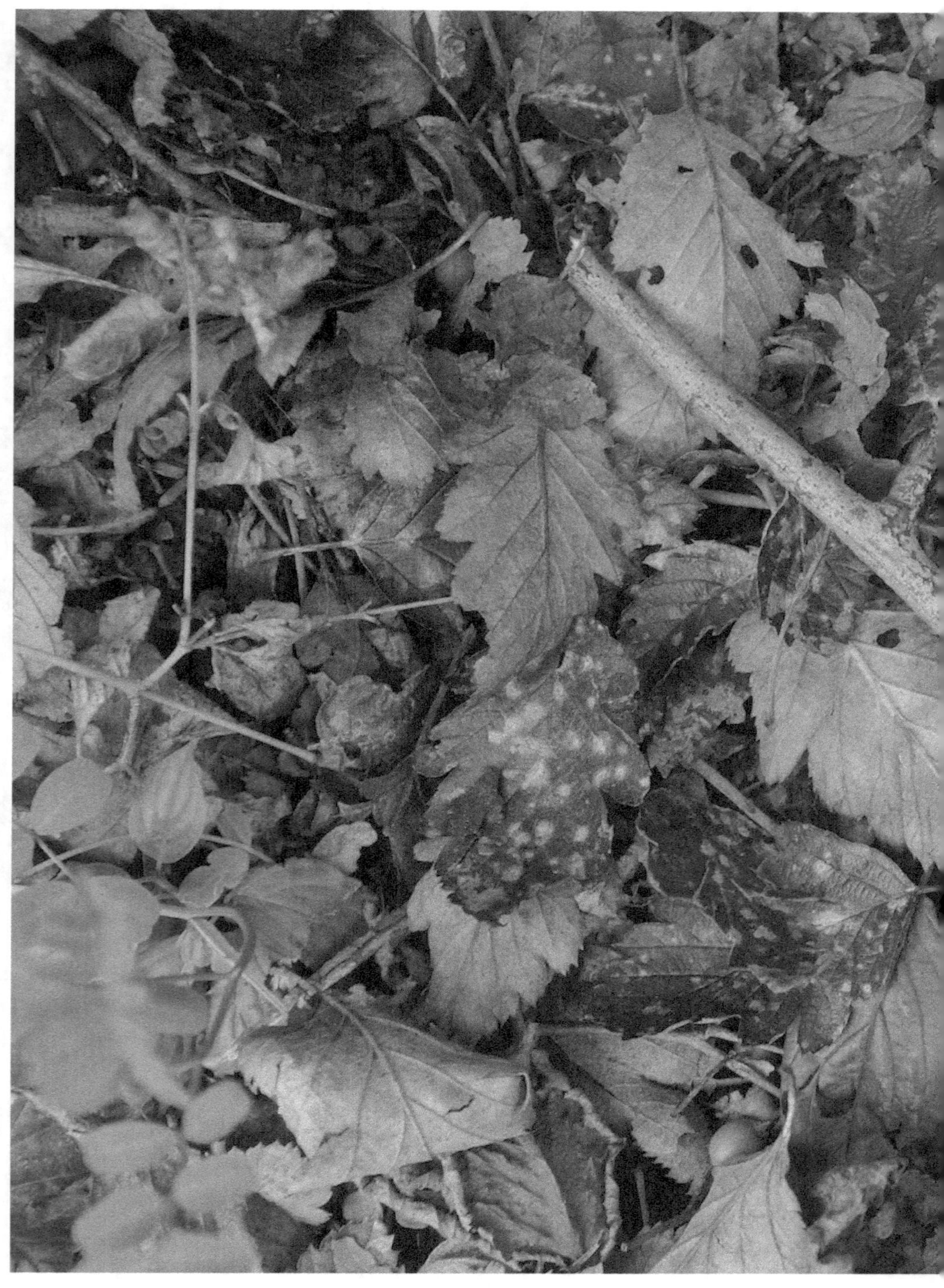

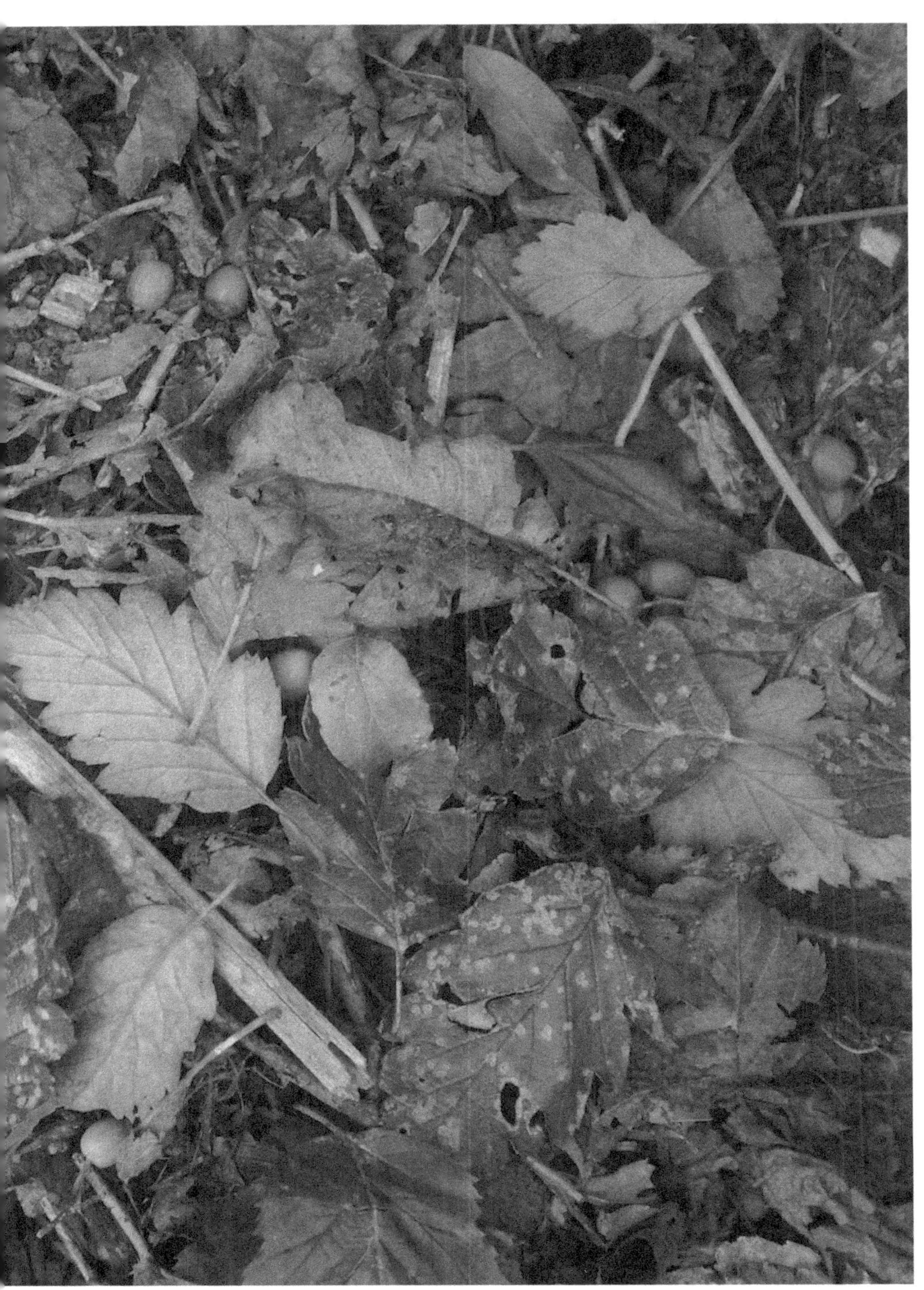

Joshua Edwards, *Hölderlin Elegy #18*, photograph, 2017

Joshua Edwards

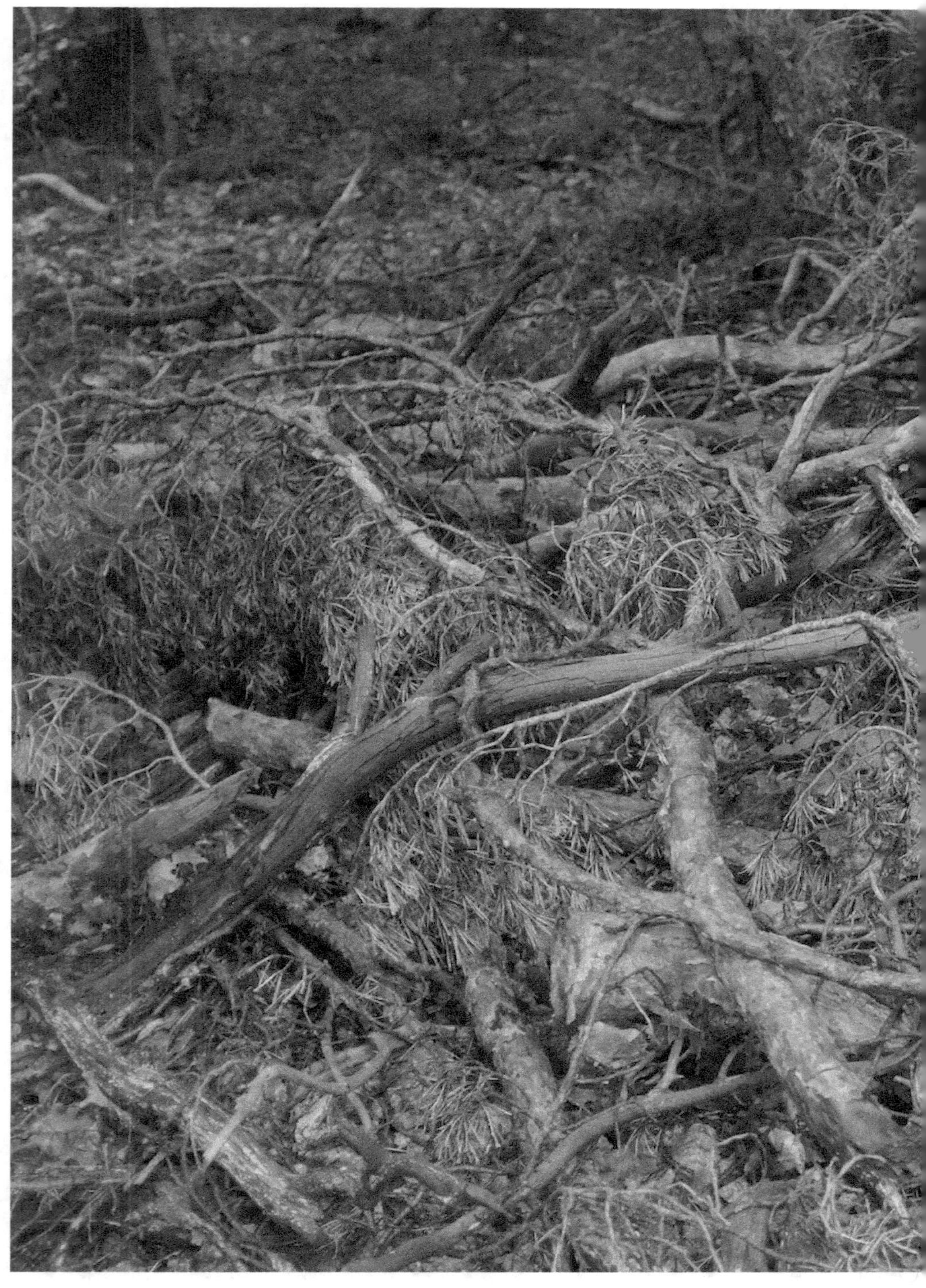

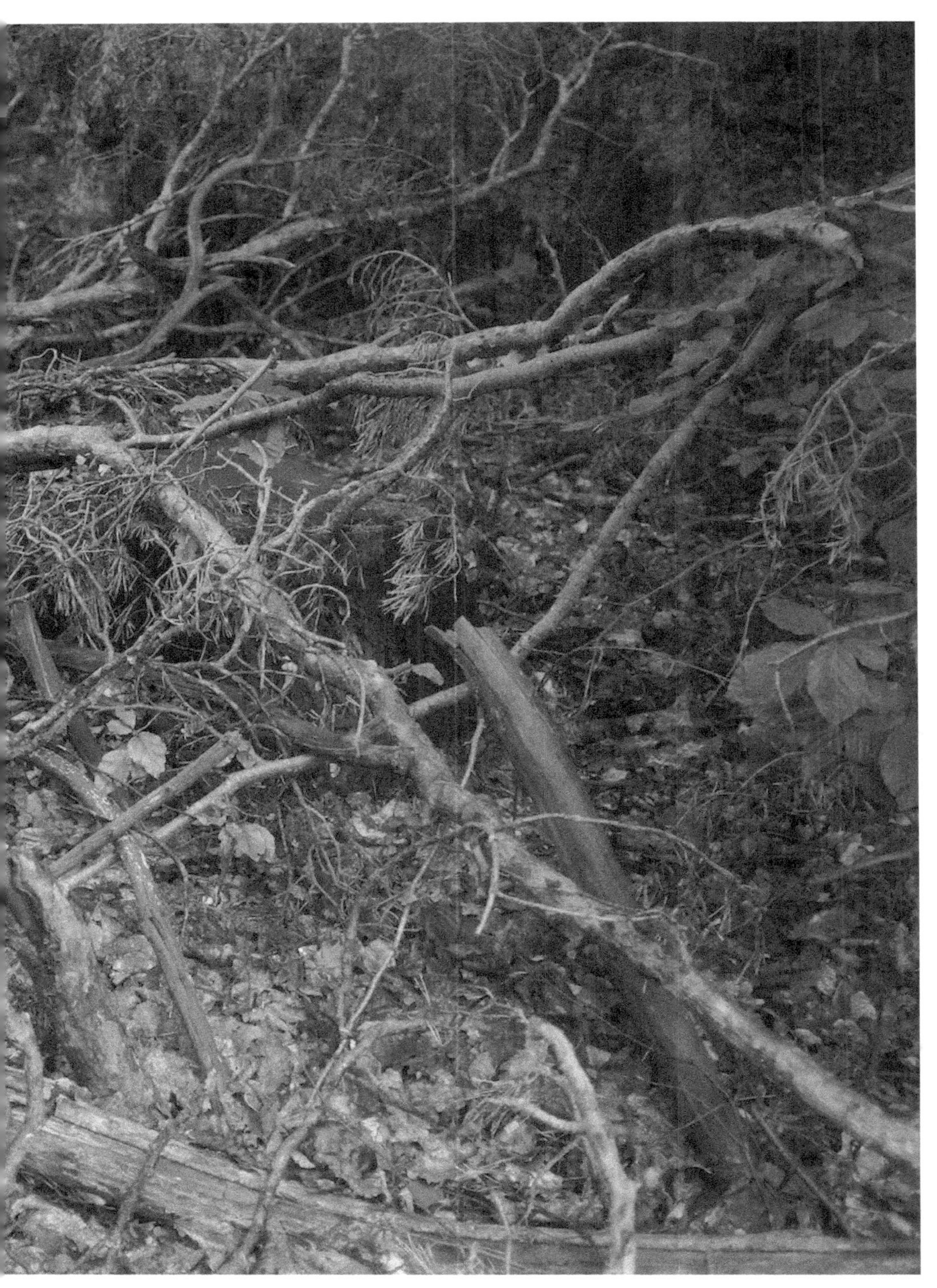

Joshua Edwards, *Hölderlin Elegy #37*, photograph, 2017

Marie Lorenz

Tide and Current Taxi on the Herring River

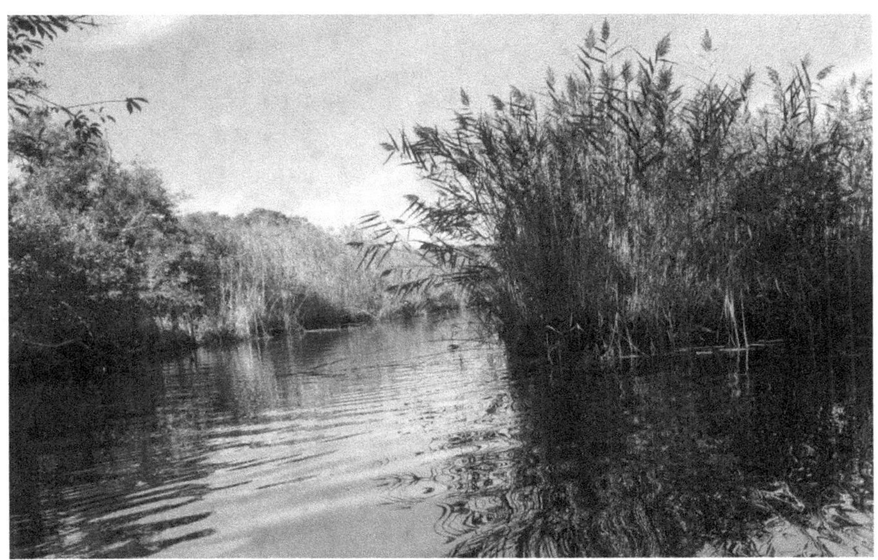

The Tide and Current Taxi is a rowboat taxi operated by Brooklyn-based artist Marie Lorenz. Each trip is planned to coincide with strong tidal currents in the New York harbor, all documented with pictures and stories at www.tideandcurrenttaxi.org. For the Researchers-in-Residence program at the Cape Cod Modern House Trust, Lorenz documented a day in the life of the Herring River, starting in the Wellfleet Harbor, and following its path back to the kettle ponds. Her blog post about the day explores ideas about conservation, stewardship, and the unintended consequences of progress, and can be found online here: http://www.tideandcurrenttaxi.org/?p=11426

Marie Lorenz

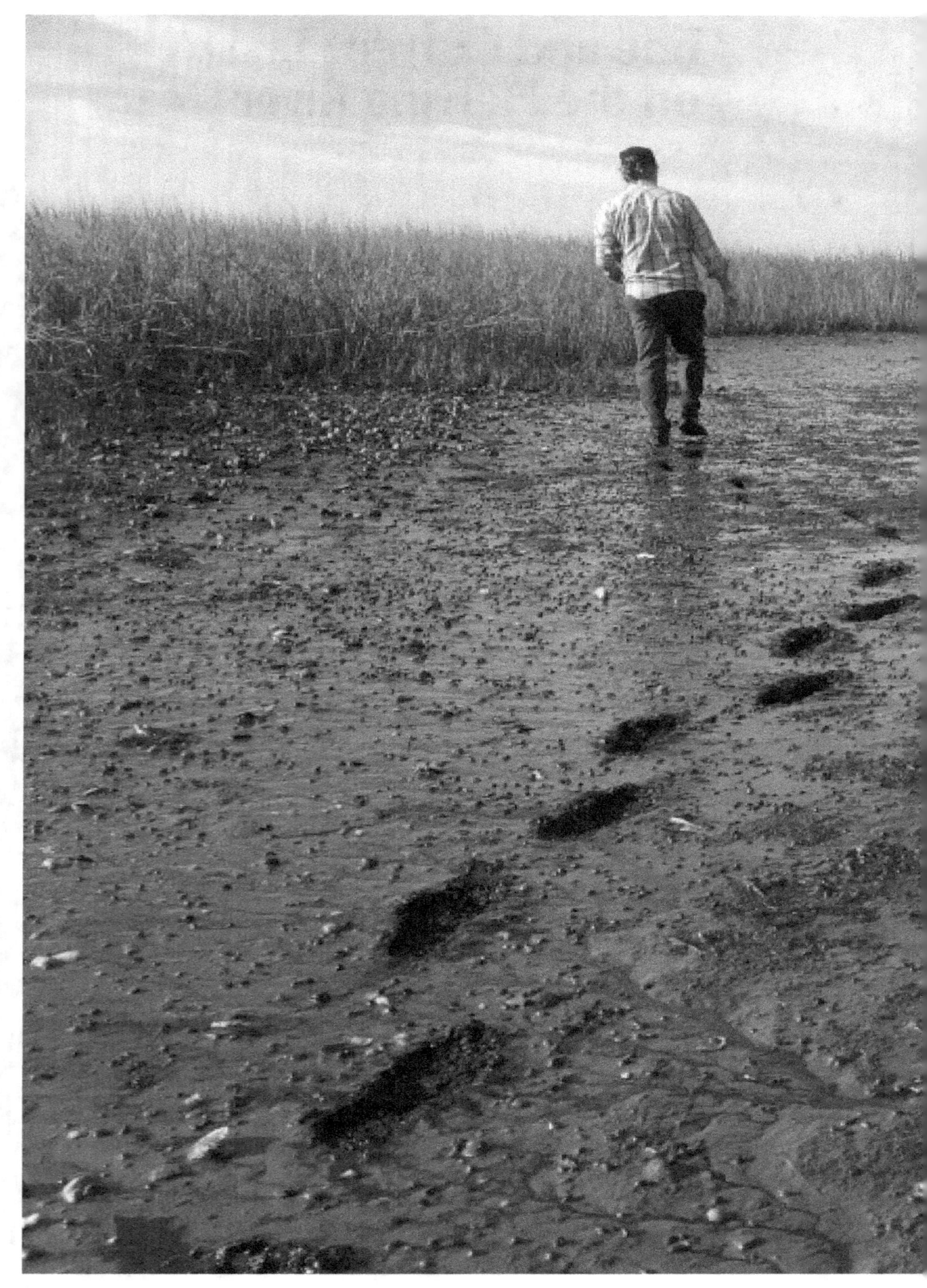

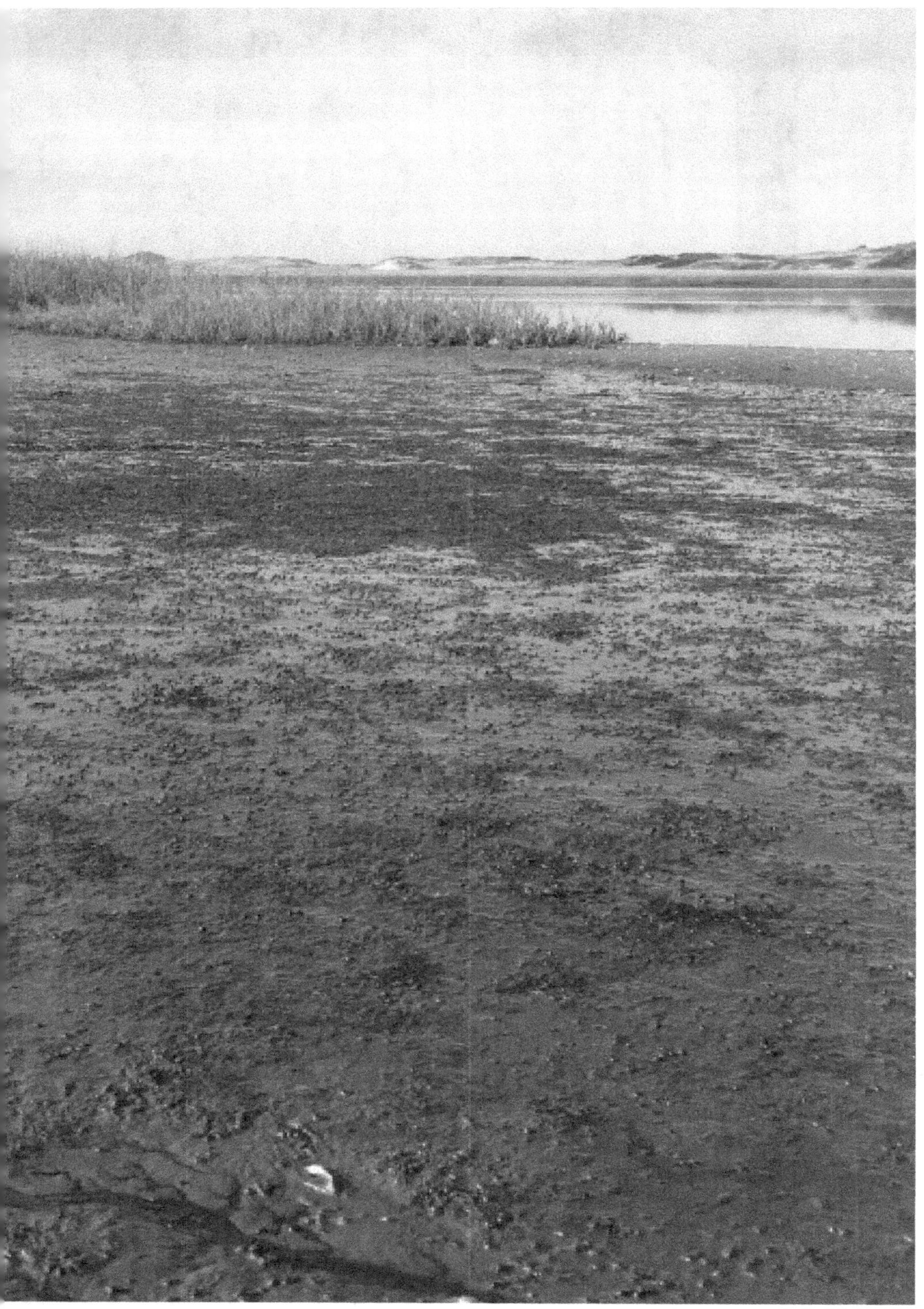

Marie Lorenz

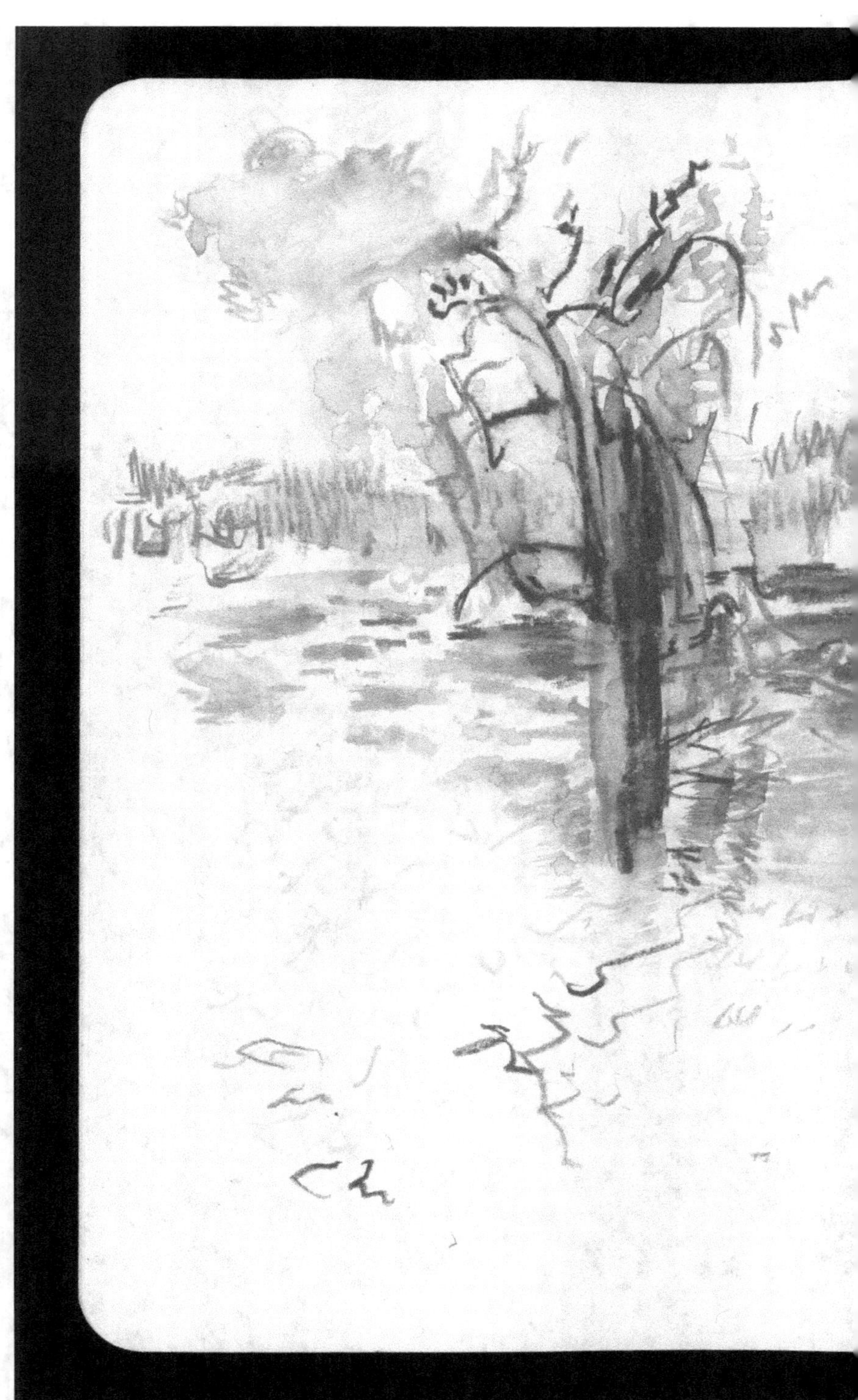

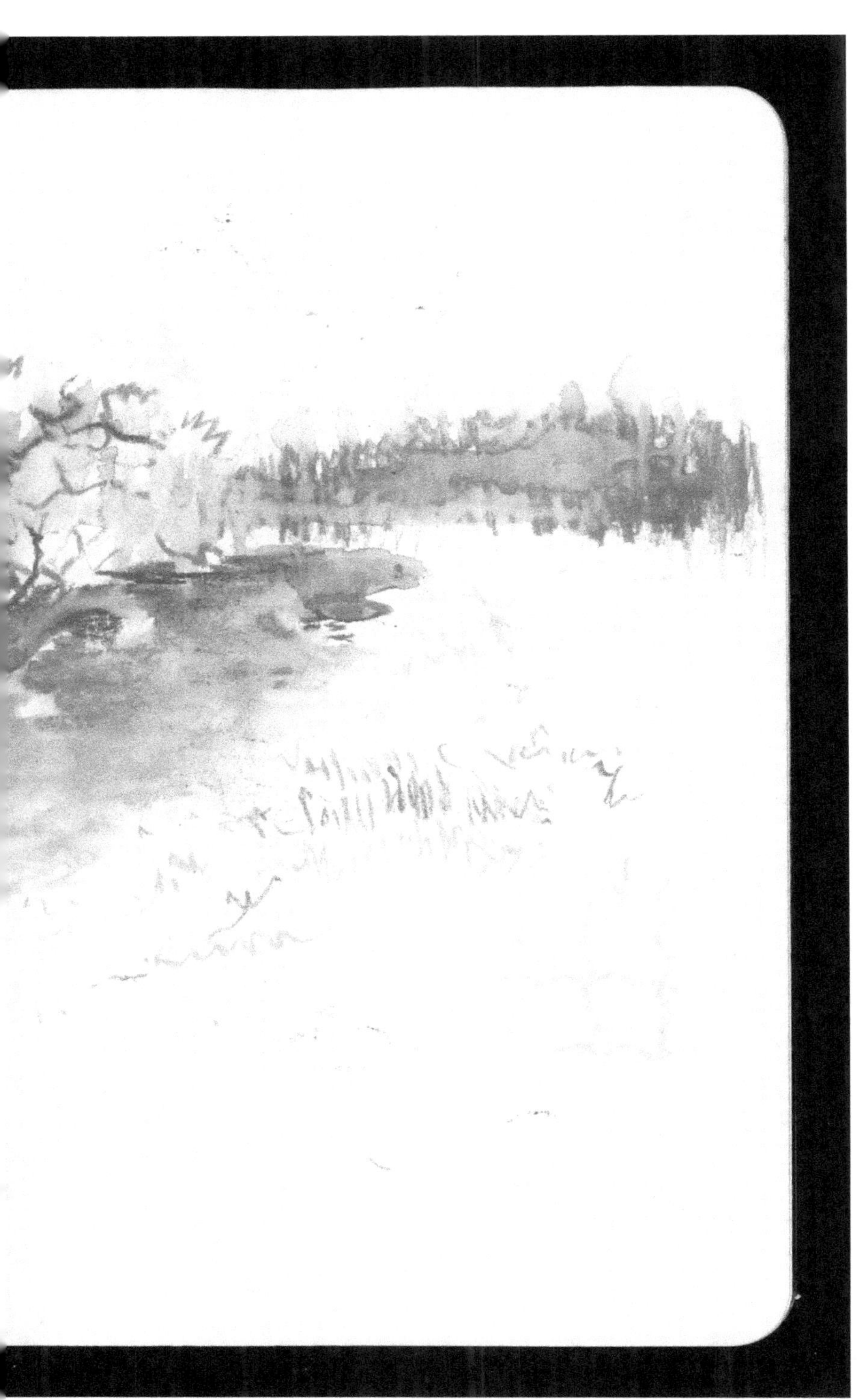

Marie Lorenz

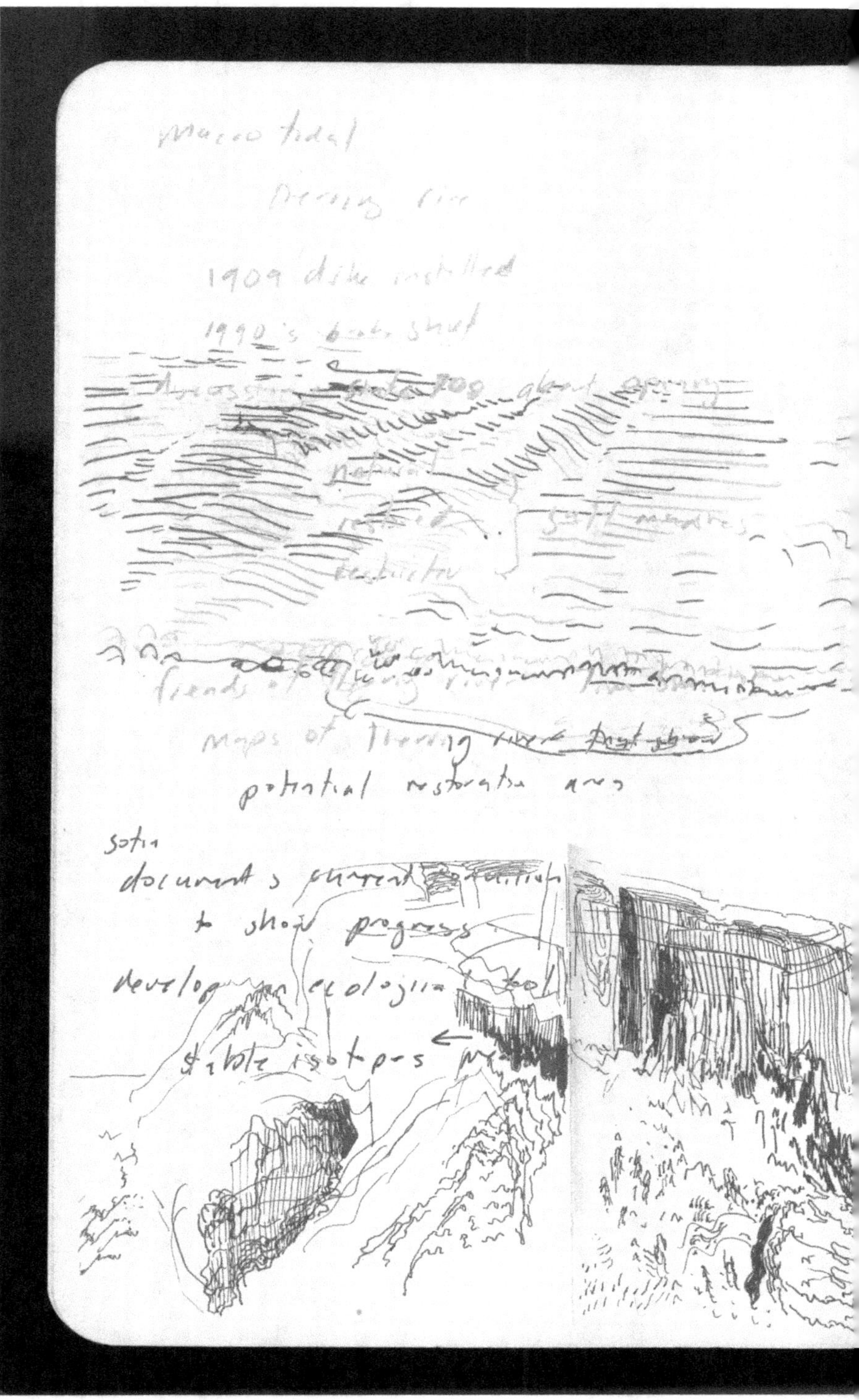

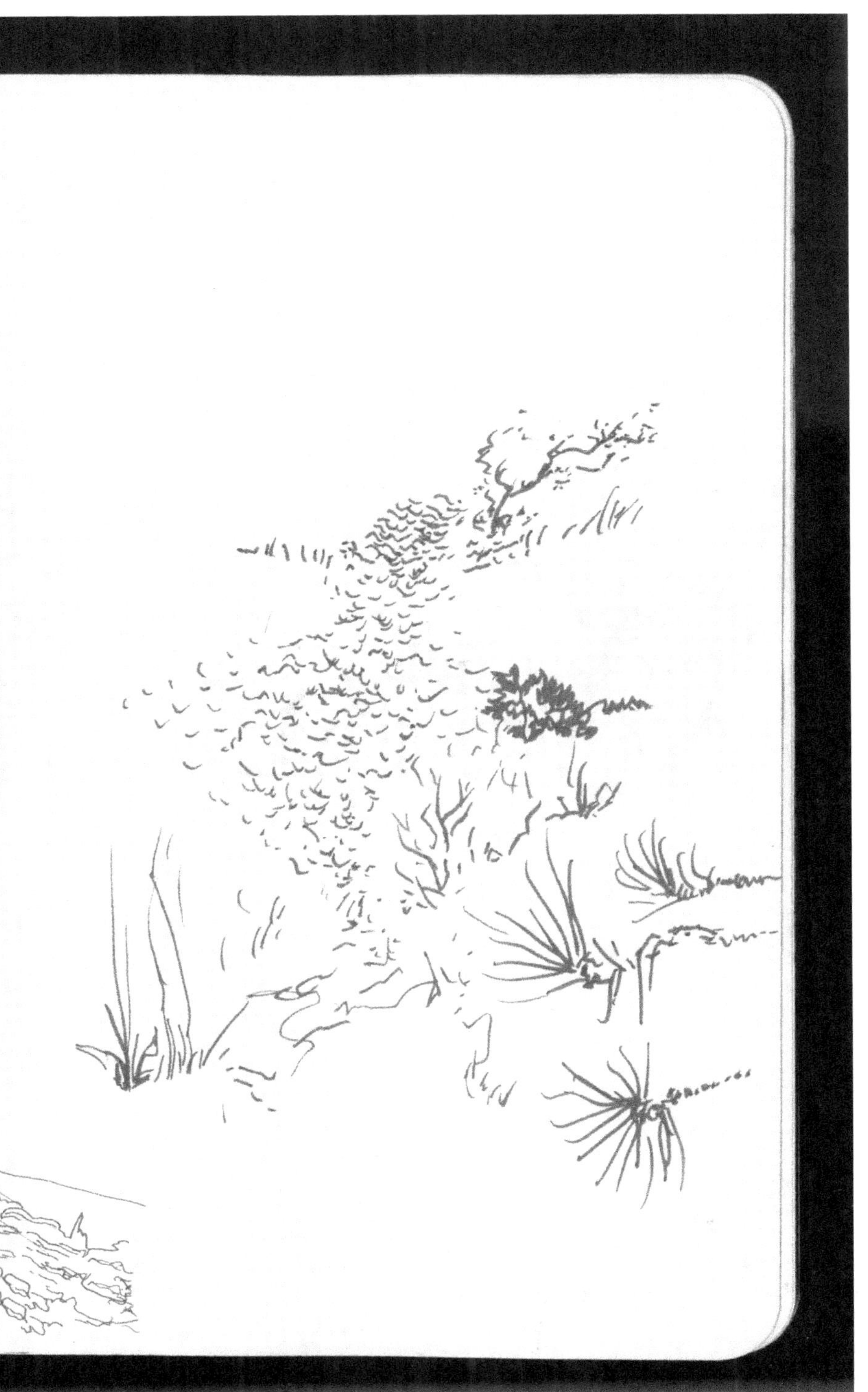

Nancy Nowacek

Curator's Note: Inspired by the intersection of nature and culture in Cape Cod, Nowacek developed two projects. The first draws parallels between the impact of microplastic particles, their chemical composition, and tongue twisters. The second postures a possible ethic of care for ocean plastics.

Mononomore

More and more plastics flow into our oceans each year — an estimated 8,000,000 tons annually. Plastics corrupt all bodies they encounter: bodies of water, bodies of sea animals, human bodies.

She sells seashells by the seashore.

Tongue twisters test the plasticity or malleability of the mouth: the ability of the tongue, teeth, lips, and breath to bend, align, and coordinate movement and position through unnatural speech formations. In this way, they corrupt the reproduction of language in the mouth, most often resulting in malaprop, or in more extreme instances, arresting the ability to speak at all.

Tongue twisters were originally designed to improve the social and economic status of the speaker by forced muscular reform — as illustrated in *My Fair Lady*. Although today we can consider this process of institutionalizing the mouth a form of biopower practiced on those who don't linguistically conform to dominant cultural standards — who aren't naturally "easy to understand," who might require more focused listening and attention. In the early 20th century, this form of rehabilitation was connected to social and economic advancement and elevation. The same can be said of plastics in the same era: they were regarded as a wonder-material and unfettered conduit of progress.

She shells sea hells by the seashore

Plastics are strings of monomers configured into polymers that exhibit extreme malleability and the ability to take any imagined form, but once hardened hold shape for 1000 years or more. As plastics begin to degrade, these same chemical compounds drift into the waterways of human and animal biology, inhibiting endocrine function and ultimately reproduction. Likewise, tongue twisters are synthetic compounds, phrases that are not naturally occurring. Focused more on sound-forming than logic-making, these engineered strings of phonemes result in absurd (or absurdly banal) statements: "How can a clam cram in a clean cream can?"

The origins of plastics and the origins of tongue twisters parallel one another in time: both began in the mid-1800s; having a major surge in the early 1900s (tongue twisters in vaudeville acts and a world of plastic in the form of bakelite accessories). For the scientists developing plastics in the early 1900s — at the same time as these linguistic therapies — the idea of a plastisphere exerting massive global damage most would have been received as an absurd proposition.

In *Monononomore*, plastics waft into common tongue twisters. Simulating cellular mutation in the mouth, they embody the ecological corruption wrought the world over by ocean plastics.

She shells PVC swells by the sleashrre

PETs

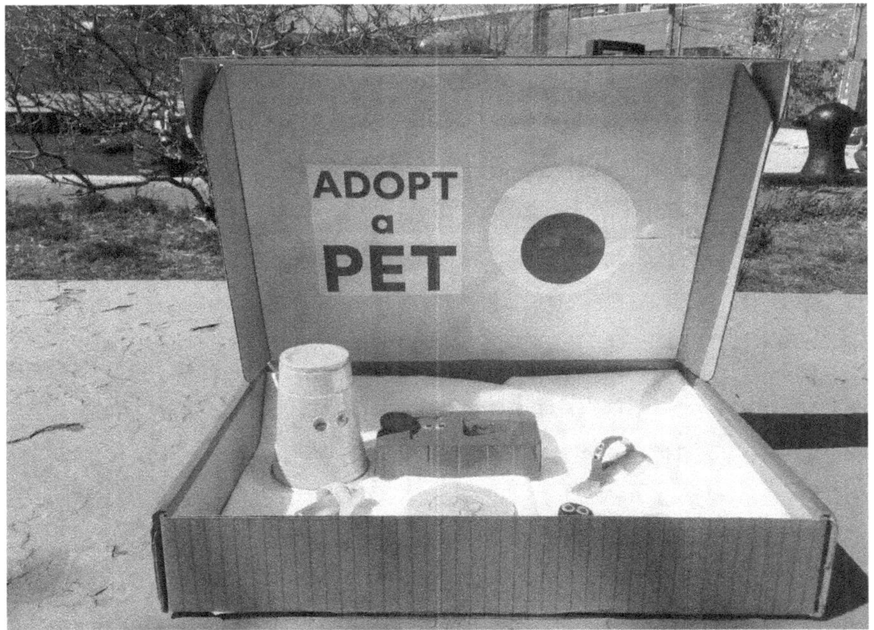

The current crisis of plastics is familiar to most Cape residents. The intimate and systematic exchange between coastal geography, oceanic life, and late capitalist consumption is also a familiar set of relationships. The damaging effects of plastic on the environment is not a difficult argument to make — especially single-use plastics — nor to be acknowledged. However, the radical forms of behavioral change necessary if our oceans are to survive may be more difficult to hear.

Before coming to Cape Cod, I thought I was aware of these conditions and arguments. As a religious plastic recycler — plastic film as well as the numbered hard plastics — I thought I was an agent of change, but my first ever walk along the beach in Wellfleet changed my understanding of the scale and scope of the problem. In a thirty-minute walk, I collected more beach plastics (of an incredible variety of size and nature) than I'd ever seen washed ashore on any beach in my lifetime of beaches. I wasn't even able to collect all the plastic I encountered — but I carried as much as I could. I bagged them up — 3 large garbage bags filled with lobster line, plastic cups, bottles, straws, buoys amongst the catch — and drove them back to Brooklyn, 21st-century seaside souvenirs.

In the months since, I have felt their presence in the bedroom closet. They have impelled me to learn more about the specifics of their far-reaching geographic and infinite existence. I now know more than I want to know about polymers and the environmental effects of their degradation. I also know that it will be impossible to eradicate all plastics from the planet.

Object-oriented ontologists have for years invested effort in shifting a human-centered approach to the world at large to an object-centered approach, where there is no hierarchy: humans are no more or no less important than any other thing. Every thing is a thing. And every thing has relationships and desires. When these ideas meet current queer theory — one that posits that we learn to love and care for non-familial others — and are applied to plastics in the environment, a proposition: can we adopt and care for the orphaned plastics that currently roam the planet via tide and current? Can we learn to love and care for them as we do our dogs and cats and birds and plants and children? Can we pledge to keep them from garbage and ocean, harm and hatred, and give them protection worthy of 1000-year lifespans?

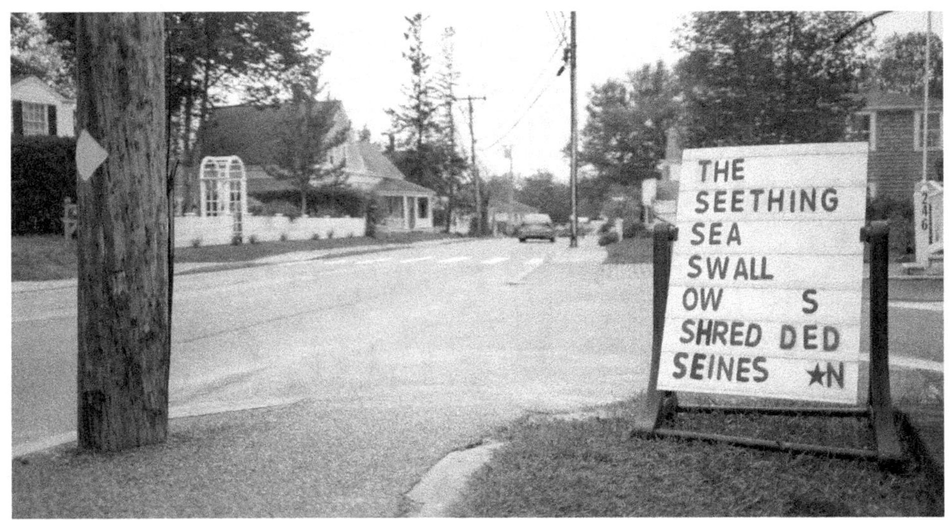

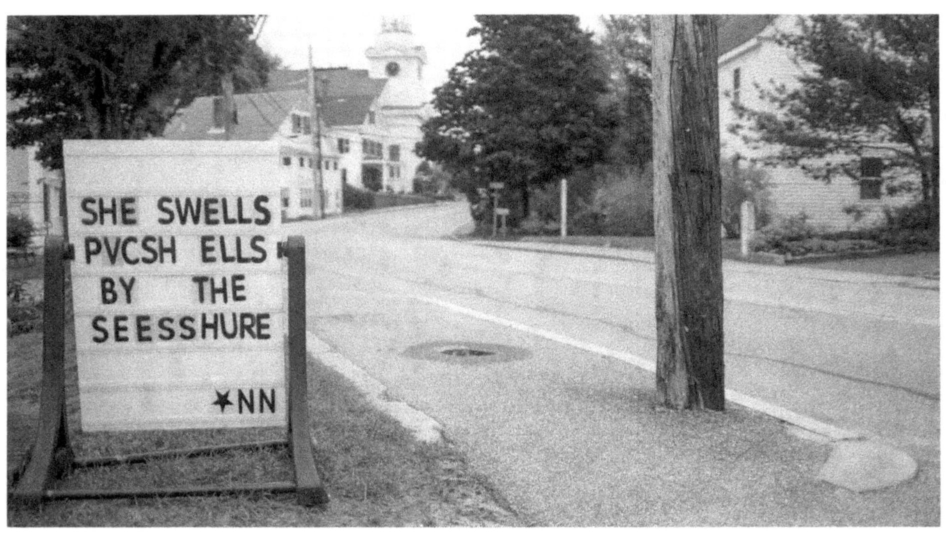

Nancy Nowacek, *Tongue Twisters*, 2018

Nancy Nowacek

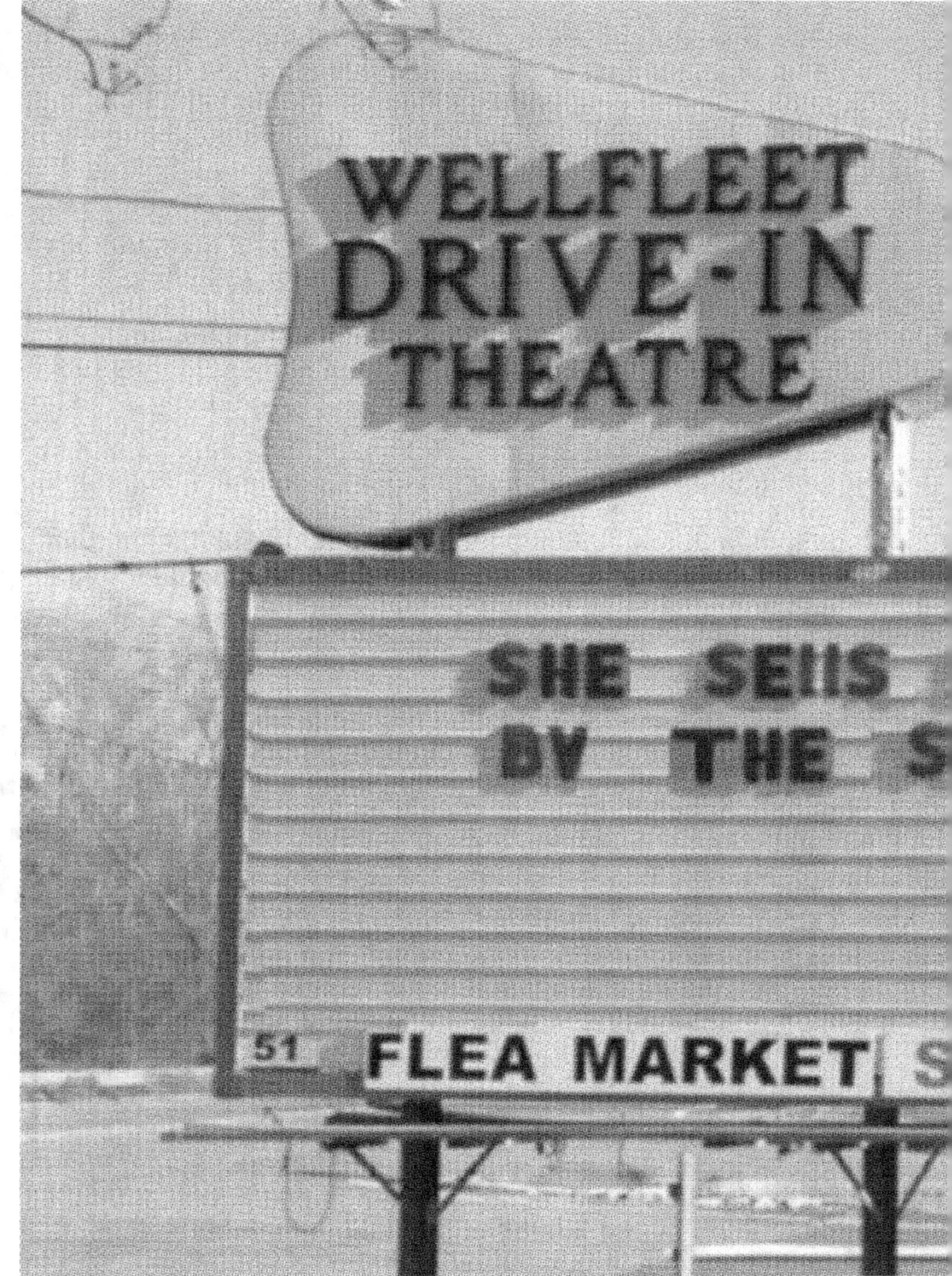

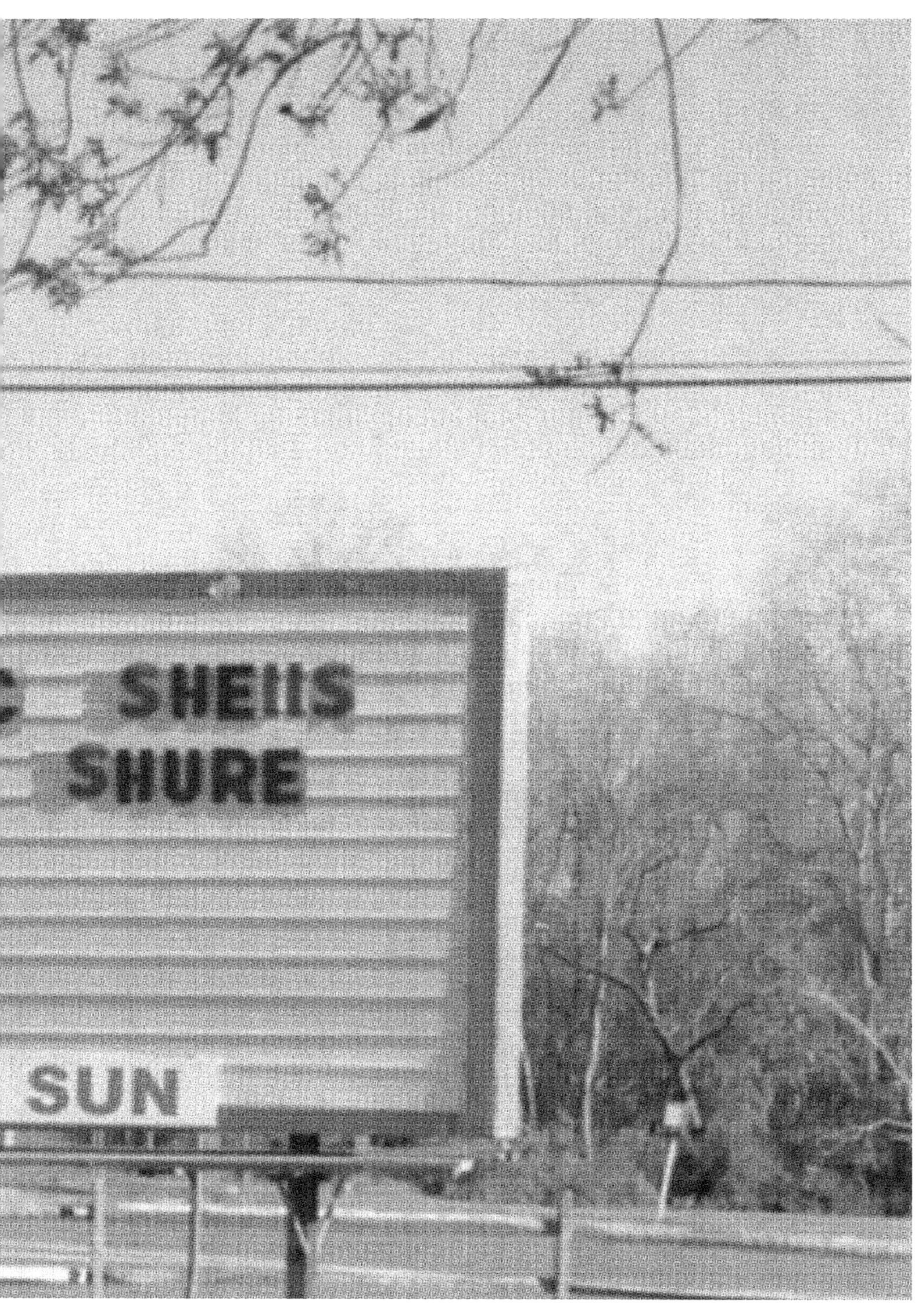

Nancy Nowacek, *Tongue Twisters*, 2018

Kendra Sullivan & Dylan Gauthier

The Institute for Ocean Art and Science (IOAS) was initiated while in residence at CCMHT as a platform for curatorial exploration, artistic research, and participatory adventures around waterways and coastlines. Inspired by the range of projects being undertaken at the NPS and the CCS, the framework of the Institute picks up on the research on urban waterways of the artist collective Mare Liberum (thefreeseas. org) and extends this work out to sea.

Fallen Ledge

The forest is dying, or so Peter and other locals fear. The moths have ravaged the leaves of the trees for two years now, and it's unclear if the trees will bloom again this year. It's already the middle of May, so by now the bloom should have happened, only everywhere you see dead trees.

Before the arrival of Europeans, the Cape was covered in a thick forest of old growth, from ocean to bay, with many small glacial ponds in between. By the 19th-century the settlers had cut down every tree to build houses, ships, and clear the land for farming. In the 20th-century, bringing back Cape Cod's forest became a priority as researchers found that the rapidly eroding dunes were now eroding more rapidly that they didn't have roots to hold them together. The roots were added by modernists who brought native saplings and their favorite trees from Europe and replanted where cows had grazed just years before. In such a short timeframe, the Cape went from forest, to pastureland, to forest again, albeit younger. These young forests of New England are a scraggly bunch. Now they may be receding again.

On the north side of the cape are the province lands, the parabolic dunes, the dune shacks. We join friends from smudge studio for tea in a nylon camping shell perched at the side of a dune they call "mother dune" because she is the largest, tallest, greatest. We wait eight minutes for tea to brew.

It is something to think that the constructed ecosystem could only exist through management, as Jedediah Purdy and others have suggested. Effective management brought nature under control, but unfortunately if the bureaucracy that manages is dismantled, will the forest survive?

The NPS Archive presents a record of all of the attempts to explain, test, prove, as well as observe, listen, record, the Outer Cape over the years since European occupation of these lands. The records are incomplete, and often include stubs of other records. Like Borges's library of babel, the full archive would have to contain information about everything that ever could be. We were initially drawn to the typology of the NPS archive. The particular aesthetic choices that had been made over the years. What Vito Acconci or Edward Tufte might have called the "aesthetics of information." As many of the studies taking place at the NPS are multi-year or even multi-decade, these forms of presentation have gone through tectonic shifts in the technologies in which they are represented, as well as the lexicon they employ to make these studies legible by the public and by other scientists.

An audio recording of pond ice melting after a deep freeze, recorded at Kugel/Gips House on January 11, 2018: https://tinyurl.com/y325c955

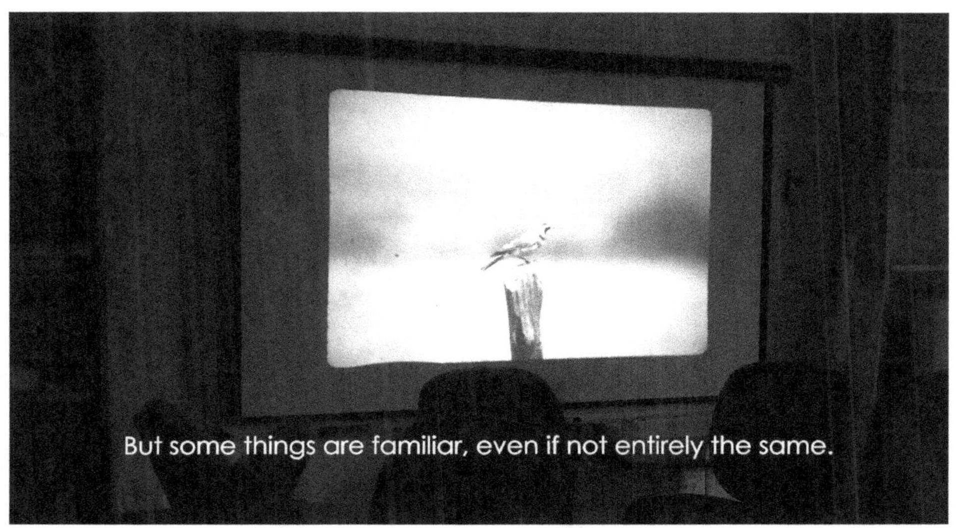

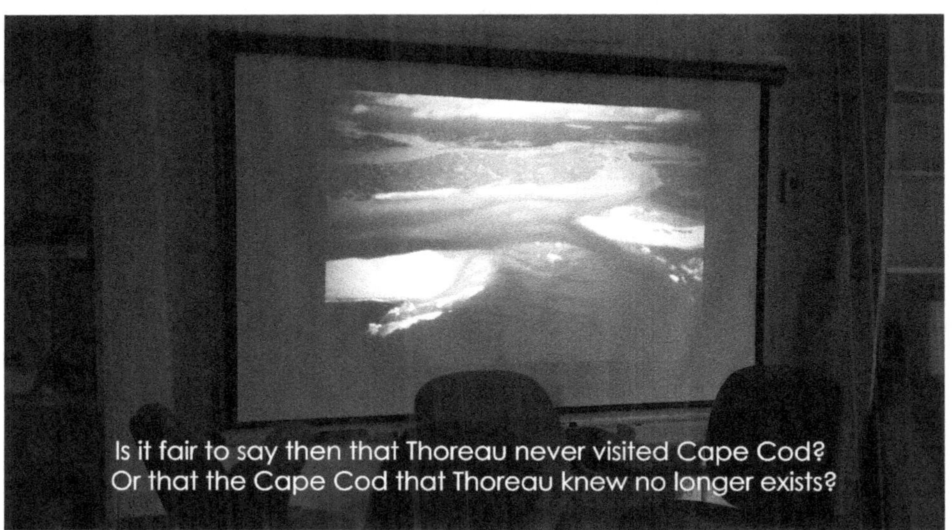

Sullivan & Gauthier, *fallen ledge,*
stills from a video (r/t: 23m10s), 2018

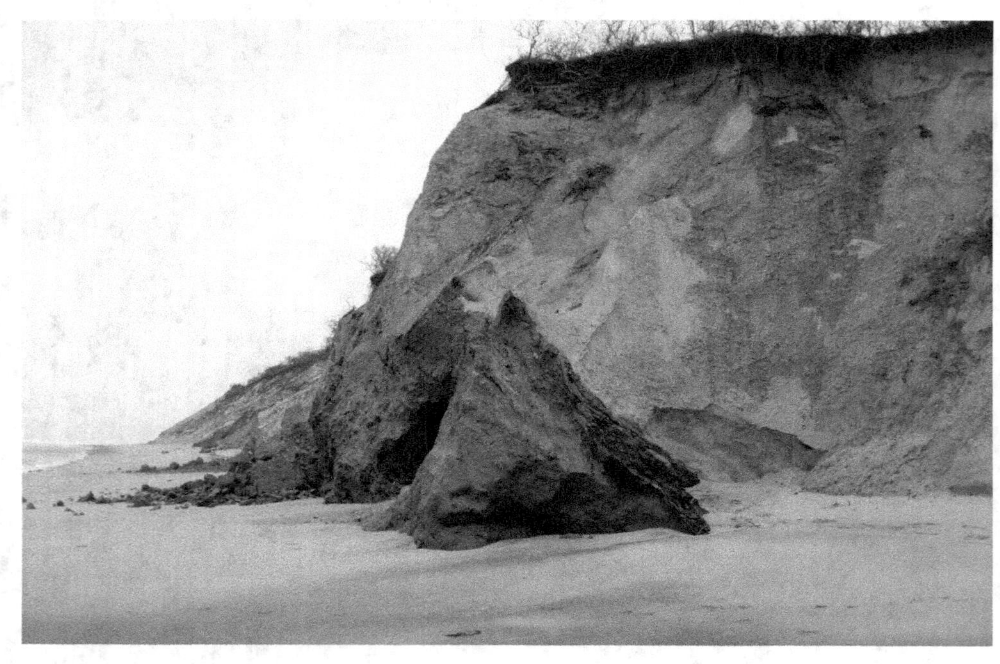

Sullivan & Gauthier, *fallen ledge*, 2017

Jeff
Williams

In 1986, the Monterey Aquarium was the first to display the Ocean Sunfish (*Mola mola*) in the US. I was fortunate to visit that very year, completely by chance, as an 8-year-old. Initially looking for sharks in the largest attraction at the aquarium, I was taken by surprise by an amorphous vertical oval wagging by. It has similar dorsal fins to a shark, but looks like the first failed attempt at something. The Sunfish was radically different than everything else in the tank, than anything I had seen before. I was most agitated by the brow of the Sunfish and how alive its eyes were, felt human. The *Mola* became my favorite fish, mine in the same way that other favorites were: pizza, the color green, the number four.

Thirty-four years later, I don't think about Sunfish ever, it's a childhood memory. Which is why when I found them dead all over Wellfleet, MA in October 2017, I was in a kind of nightmarish shock. First, a well picked over and dried up corpse on the beach, where I wasn't certain what I was looking at until days later. Then the fin of a large Mola thrashing around as it was beached near the Herring River dam. The local fisherman reassured me that at 500–1000 pounds, nothing could be done. Marie Lorenz and I rowed out to the area at low tide, trekked through the mud to find out what happened to the Sunfish, hoping it somehow freed itself.

What we encountered is illustrated in the drawing, cell phone for scale. A 5 foot long, 6 foot tall, 1 foot wide freshly asphyxiated Sunfish. We pretended to be scientific about the find, taking measurements and documenting the circumstances of its death. But really it was a morbid curiosity and a sincere empathy for something I had made part of my developing identity. We documented it as thoroughly as possible, thinking maybe some of our data could be useful to the National Parks scientists working in Wellfleet.

We left the site as the tide came in. As we rowed, looking to move on, we saw what appeared to be a birch tree branch floating in the water. As we paddled closer, the tree branch transformed in our minds. It was a quick flash from branch to a large Mola corpse floating upside down with its nose up. At this point what we eventually found out from the park scientists became clear. This is a massive die-off of the planet's heaviest bony fish. Due to changes in climate, warmer waters keep the Sunfish from migrating when they should and then there is a shift in ocean temperature, with that shift a drop in oxygen levels leading to death.

Jeff Williams

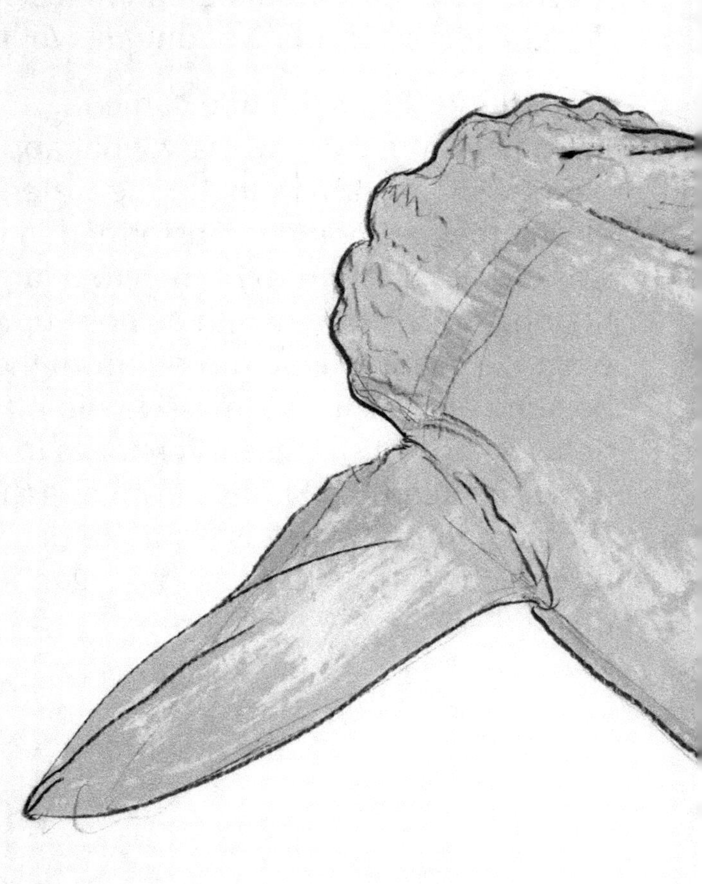

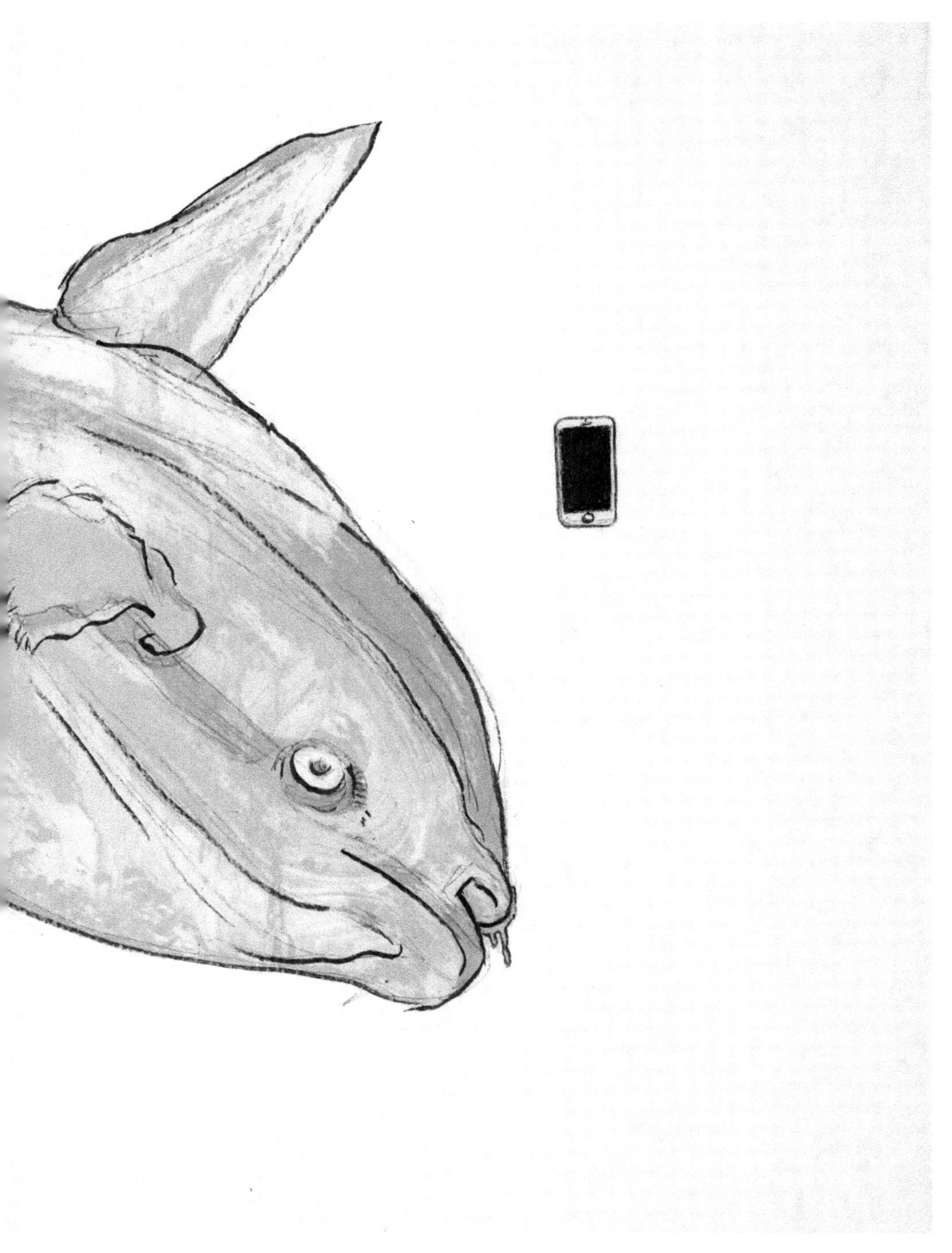

Jeff Williams, *Sunfish*, 2018

Lynn
Xu

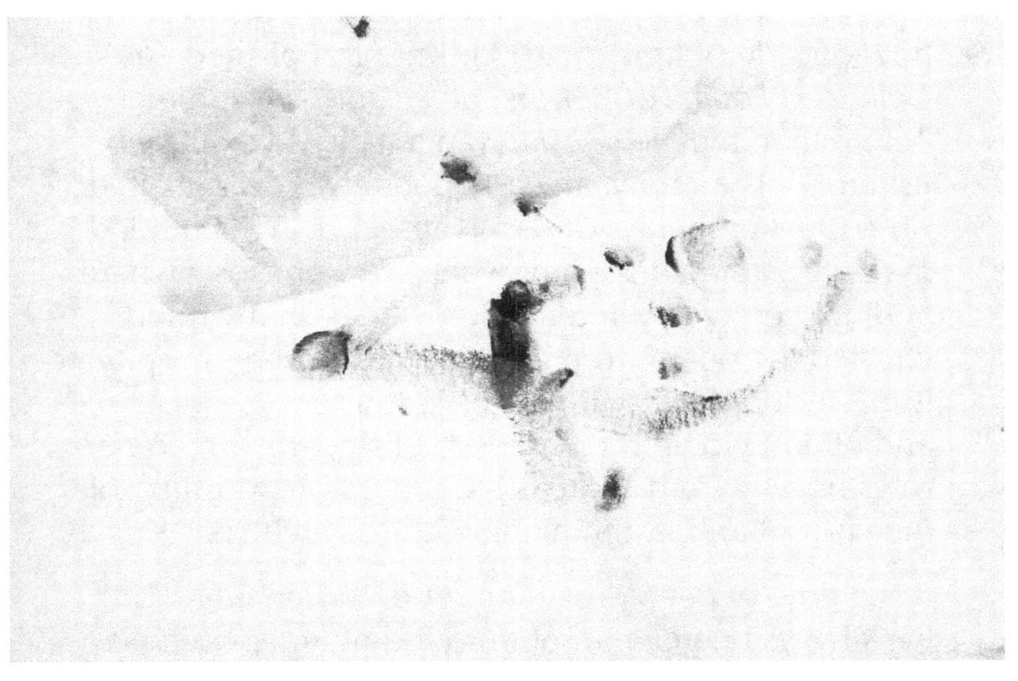

Issa Edwards, *Cape Sea*, 2018

We spent our time mainly at the Weidlinger House lifted ten feet in the air by a thicket of pine. During the day, I worked in the small room facing Higgins Pond typing poems I'd been muddling (middling) over about the endless aperture of birth while Josh (my husband) took Issa (our daughter) into town. In the night, we would cook with Kendra and Dylan (who were also staying at Weidlinger) or convene with Peter, Mark and the others at Hatch or Kugel/Gips. Somehow, at this time, it was always sunset. Or, the sun was always just setting or about to set, and there was always wine.

I am rereading Peter's book this morning and it strikes me (as it does always) how much these experiments in building (and building as/with living) returns to or

is resolved by a thinking with kinship, which is somehow outside of time. In 2003, Knopf published *The
Collected Poems of Robert Lowell* and, the summer
before that, the *New Yorker* ran a feature which published, in its entirety, an early poem by Lowell called
"The Quaker's Graveyard in Nantucket," which Kendra recited to me one night when we were somewhere
and not yet twenty, a recitation which (in my mind)
wrested the poem from itself and, as it were, in spite
itself, restored the wildness of its composition. Later
and often I would remember it, this poem, which bor-
rows heavily from Thoreau's *Cape Cod* (exposition of
the corpse) and is a thinking with the archive.

It is a time of deep dreaming. And, for me, Kendra
has always been a part of this kind of time, which is
to say: I am interested in the way ideas move not as
ideas but as kin. In his proposal to "translate Utopia
into action," Moholy-Nagy emphasizes the impor-
tance of living together: "They [the scientists, sociol-
ogists, artist, writers, musicians, technicians, and
craftsmen] would work either for a long or limited
period of time together, in daily contact, in their stu-
dios and laboratories." In this thinking, space is itself
a movement of the mind and there is something else
that happens (that cannot actually be recapitulated by
and/or as ideas) when we are trying, as Barthes says,
to live alone together.

So, when we were thinking about what to make for
our time there, Josh and I wanted to create something
that returns the space to itself, to the houses, the sea,
the research, and history of place. We wanted to find
a way (and, in a way, to think with Goethe's idea of

observation as experiment) to borrow reading for listening and listening, a way to hear space (as history, as archive, as light and shadow) and — as it were — the various ways in which kinship can be experienced and thought.

Lynn Xu

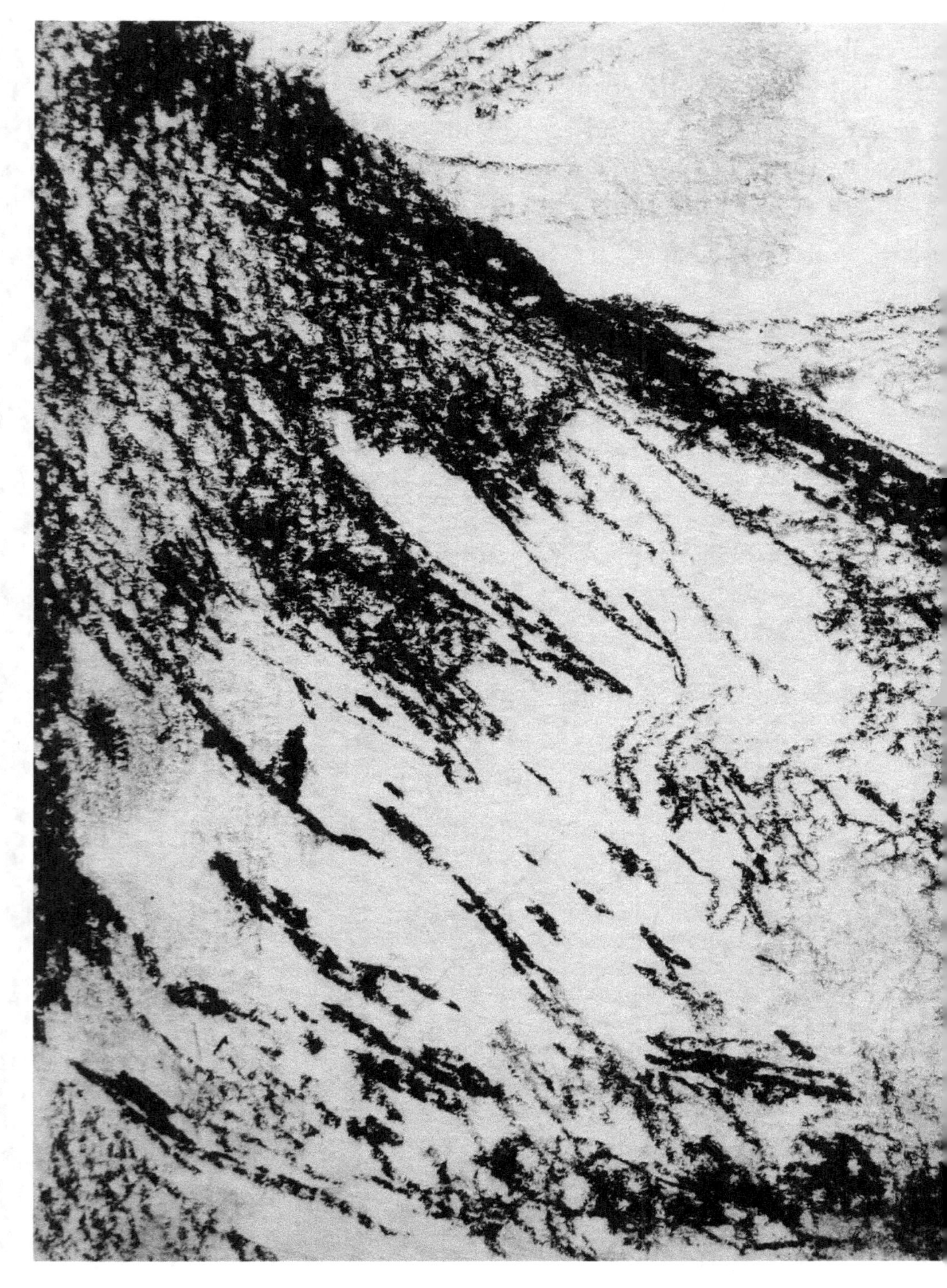

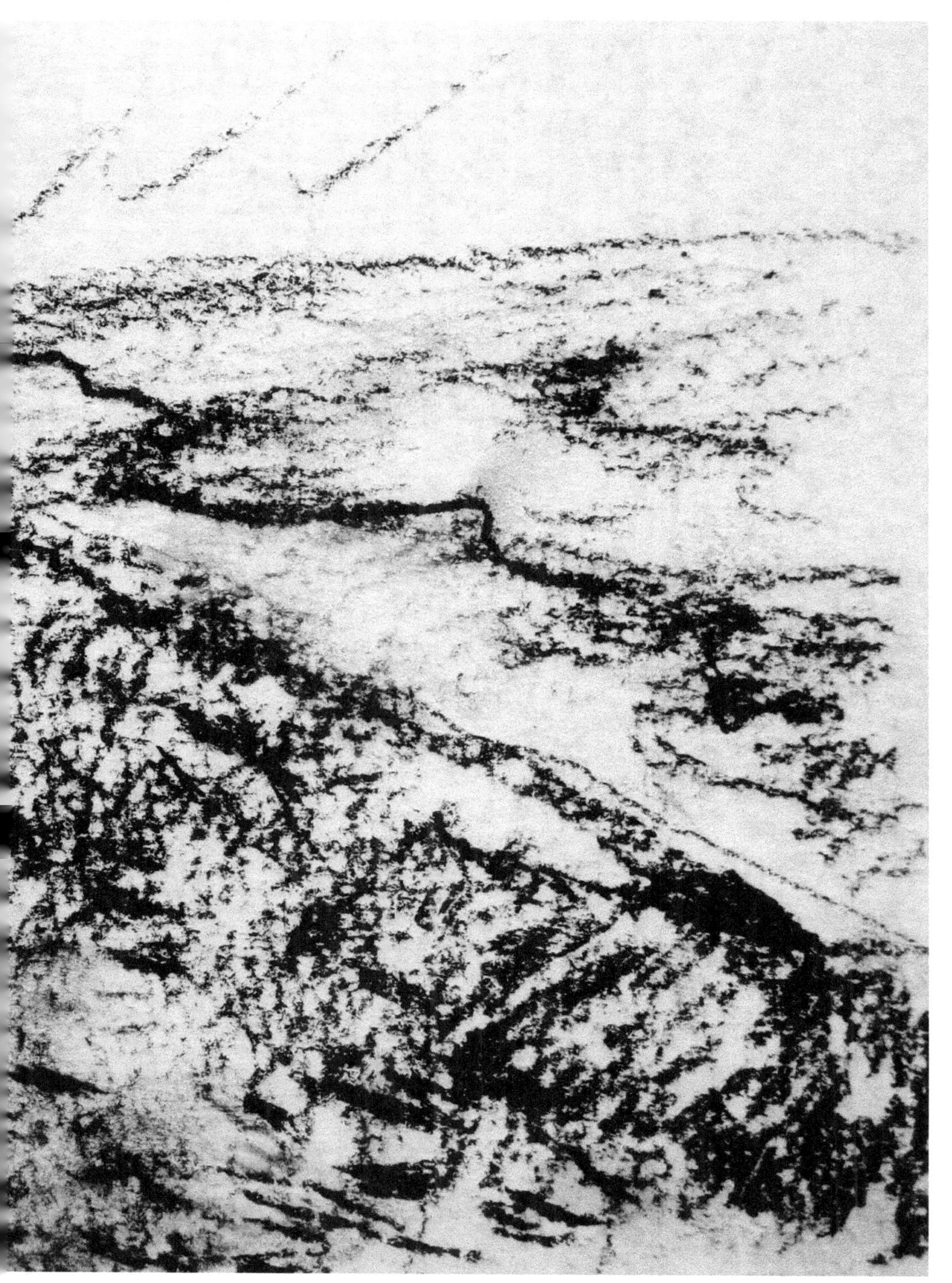

Lynn Xu, *Cape Sea 1*, 2018

Lynn Xu

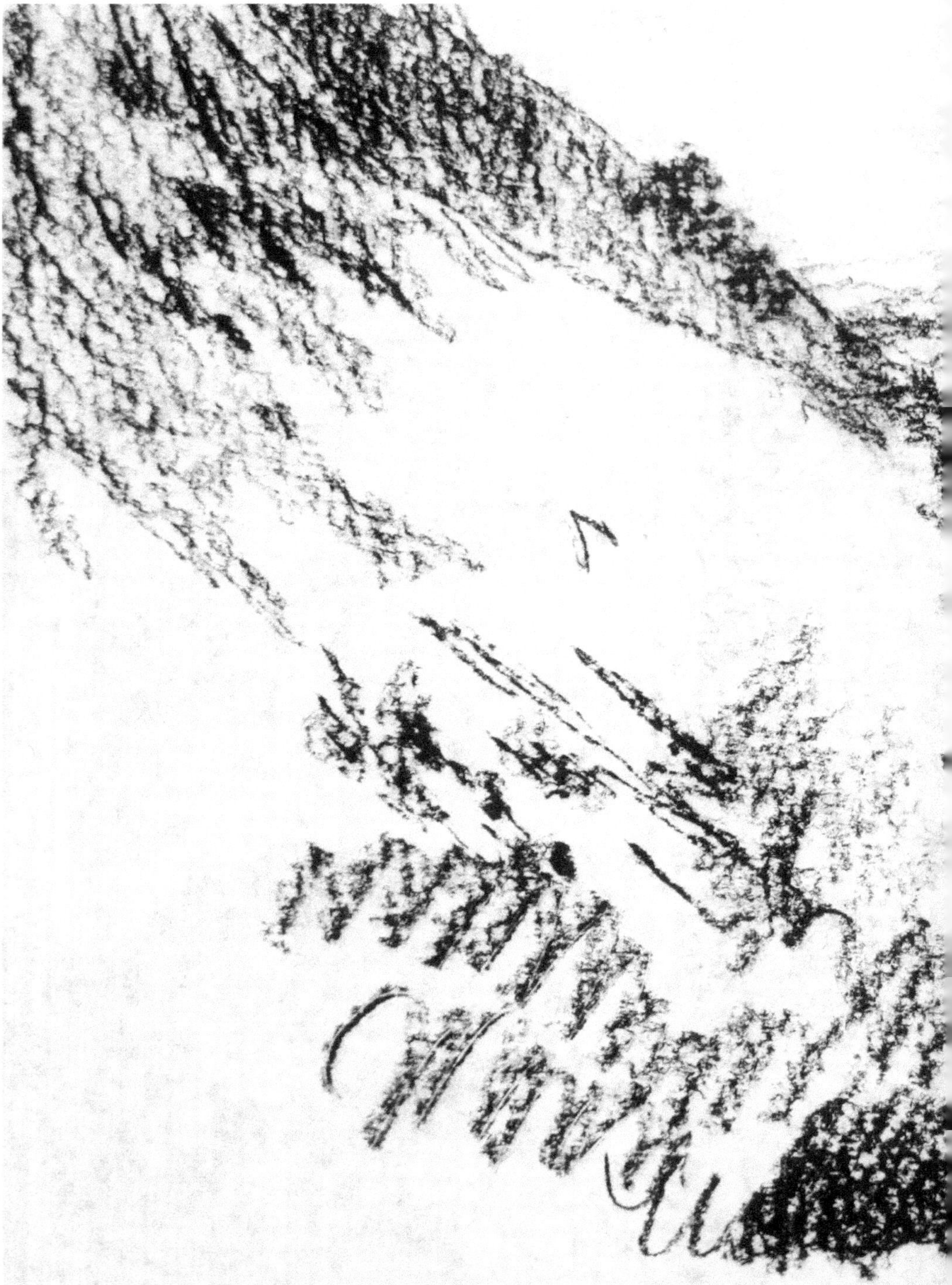

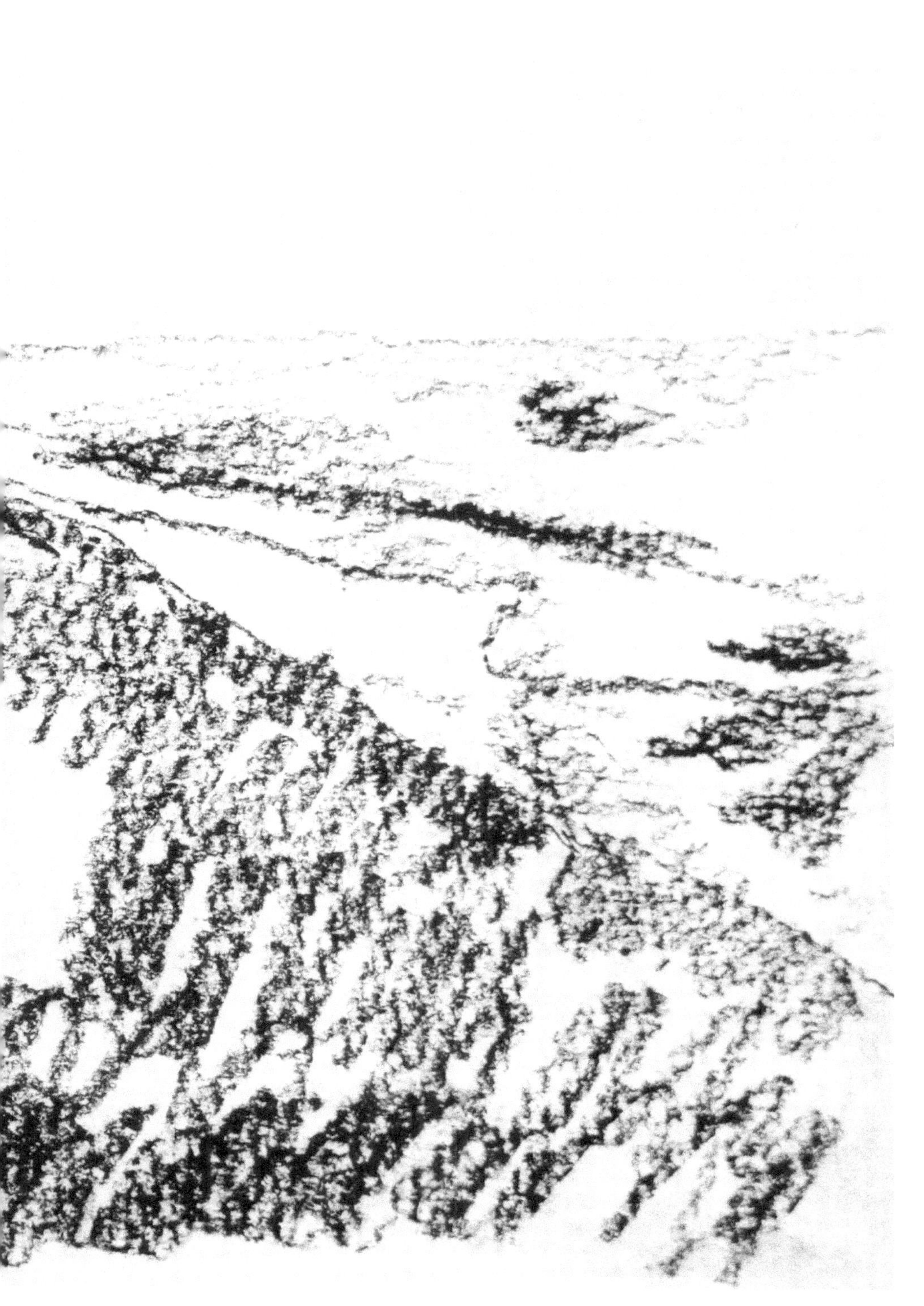

Lynn Xu, *Cape Sea 2*, 2018

Lynn Xu

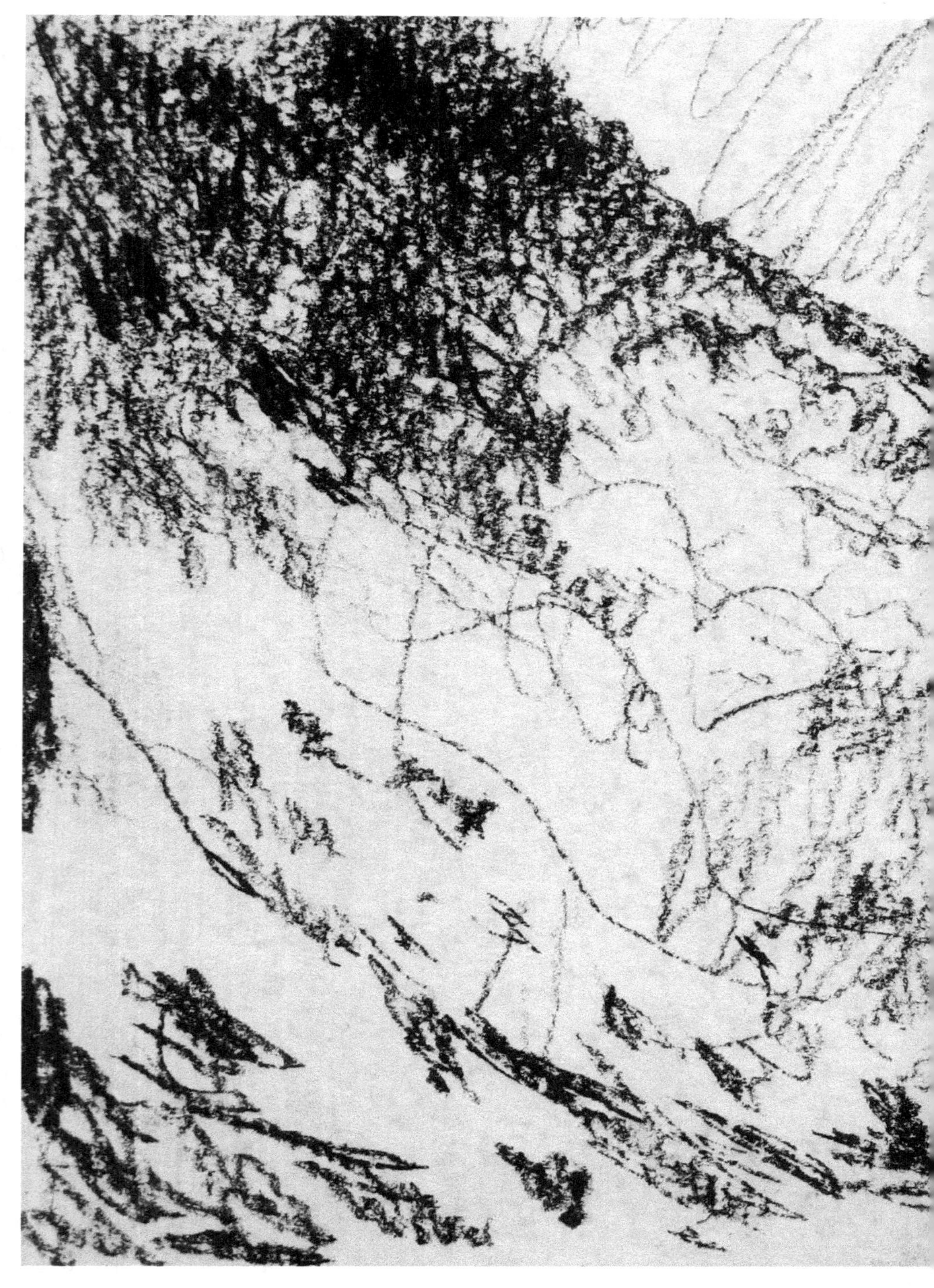

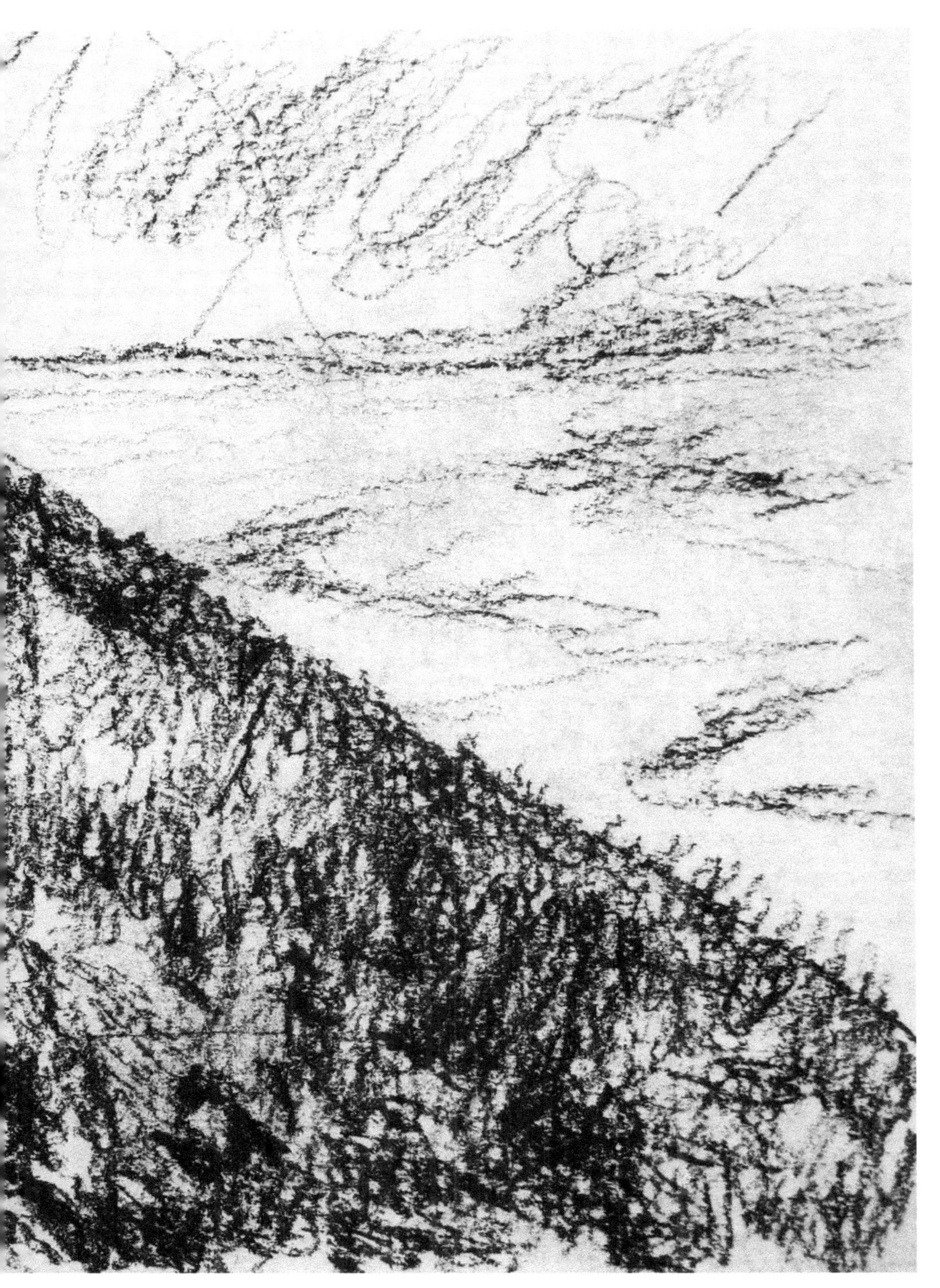

Lynn Xu, *Cape Sea 3*, 2018

Marina Zurkow

Right whale identification relies on the distinct pattern, known as a callosity, that each whale displays like a blazon on the back of their head. These are rough skin patches — callouses. Whalers called them "bonnets." Each whale is born with their callous-formation, which grows pitted and grooved like volcanic terrain over time. Callosities would not be visible were it not for the species of cyamids who colonize them, eating algae and the whale's sloughing outer skin.

Whalers used to think these cyamids were lice, and the name stuck ("whale louse") but they are actually amphipod crustaceans. These cyamids are white or yellowish, or orange, whereas the callosities are gray like the rest of the right whale. In effect, the cyamids allow us to uniquely identify each whale, which we do, from surveying airplanes. This identification is important to us humans, in order to track, quantify, characterize — and some might suggest care more about — the whales and their success or demise as a species. One could say the cyamids are producing signs that humans want to read. In fact, it's a nuanced set of signs:

> White bonnets: the whale is healthy.

> Orange bonnets: the whale is ill, injured, or dying.

The poetry of this isn't lost on anyone working in the field: cyamid species move around and relocate when the right whale is sick: *C. erraticus* move out of their genital folds and creases, and migrate into the wounds, signing sickness.

On each right whale around 5000 *Cyamus ovalis* coat the callosities and give them their white color. In the spaces between the raised callosities live around 500 *C. gracilis*. On adult whales approximately 2000 *C. erraticus* live in the genital and mammary slits. *C. erraticus* is highly mobile though often occupying wounds, and living in large concentrations on the heads of young calves. Of these *C. gracilis* is the smallest with ~6mm long adults and with the other two species measuring ~12-15mm long as adults. (Heupel)

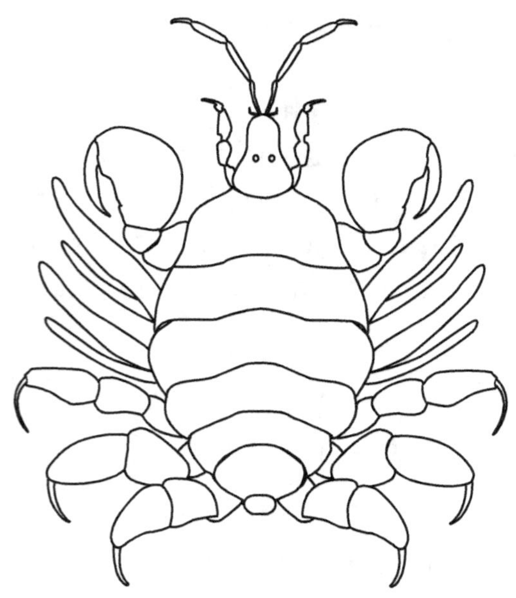

Cyamid

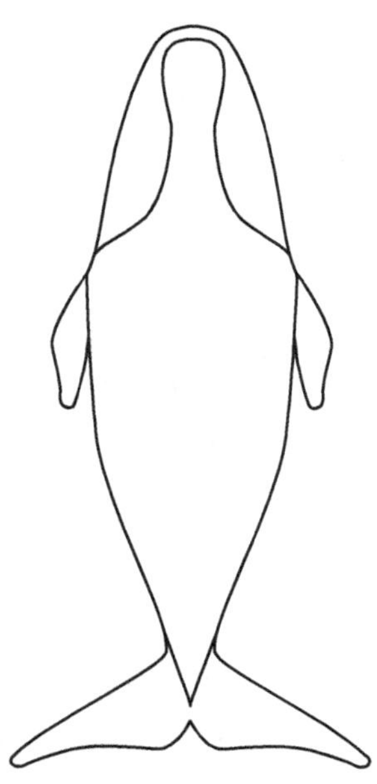

North Atlantic right whale

Cyamids spend all phases of their life cycle on their cetacean hosts. The cyamids who live on North Atlantic right whales know no other species or environment. They can't swim. They are passed from whale to whale — for instance, from a mother to calf, or while mating.

After spending so much time thinking about, drawing, and positioning cyamids in their uniquely identifiable callosity patterns on right whale diagrams, I equally feel sadness for the loss of these tiny crustacea as for their enormous, charismatic hosts. When I browse the right whale catalog (from which I have been drawing) I see both an individually identified whale and its cyamid symbionts; when the whale data states "last seen" or "death year," I experience the tensions between our capacity to care, to not care, to prefer nameable species, to shun the nameless or "uncharismatic" swarm. These cyamid portraits were uncomfortable to assemble. I could physically feel the otherness of the swarm as I assembled the bonnet groupings, for these are animals, and not simply signs.

These banners honor a colony of commensal animals who, coincidental to their lives on the whale, inadvertently "sign" the whale's individuality to us human creatures. We who love both science and story tend to care more when we can identify individuals; the swarm of crustaceans, on the other hand, is grotesque because their form and their mass behavior is so alien to us. The cyamids perform a beautiful gift with their accidental labor of signing to us, helping us care about marine creatures who, ironically, are too large and submerged for humans to identify or interface with in any other way than through both the aid of tiny crustaceans and the distancing means of aerial photography.

I feel compassion for both right whale and *C. ovalis, C. gracilis,* and *C. erraticus*, whose numbers are declining, who all may very well disappear in our lifetimes from the earth (ocean), if we don't significantly (there's that word again, sign/significance) change our fishing and shipping practices that cause net entanglement, marine noise pollution, and ship-related injuries. Both right whales and their cyamid symbionts deserve to be honored and preserved, advocated for. Part of this advocacy is toward a change of mindset: find kinship with the horde, they who don't speak, but who give us the whales' names with which we quantify, identify (with), and defend.

Sources:

"North Atlantic Right Whale Catalog." North Atlantic Right Whale Catalog. New England Aquarium. http://rw-catalog.neaq.org/.

Heupel, Eric. "Right Whale Lice." The Other 95 Percent: An Appreciation of the Underappreciated Majority of Life , September 1, 2008. http://other95.blogspot.com/2008/09/right-whale-lice.html.

Kaliszewska, Zofia A., et al. "Population Histories of Right Whales (Cetacea: Eubalaena) Inferred from Mitochondrial Sequence Diversities and Divergences of Their Whale Lice (Amphipoda: Cyamus)." Molecular Ecology 14, no. 11 (2005): 3439–56. https://doi.org/10.1111/j.1365-294x.2005.02664.x.

Würsig, Bernd G., J. G. M. Thewissen, and Kit M. Kovacs. Encyclopedia of Marine Mammals. Elsevier, 2018.

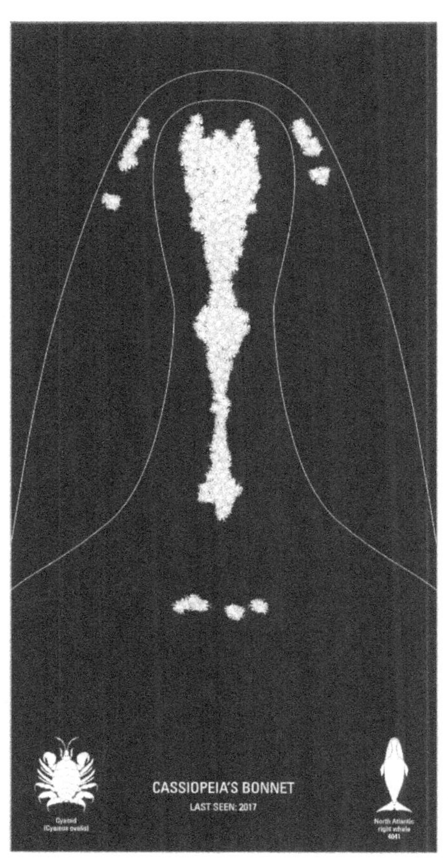

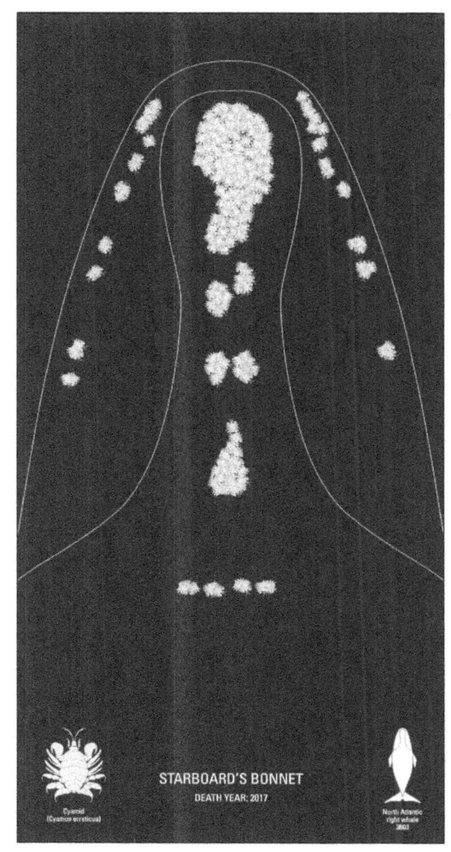

Marina Zurkow, *A Swarm is my Bonnet*
Nylon banners, 42" x 84" each 2018

Exhibition Images

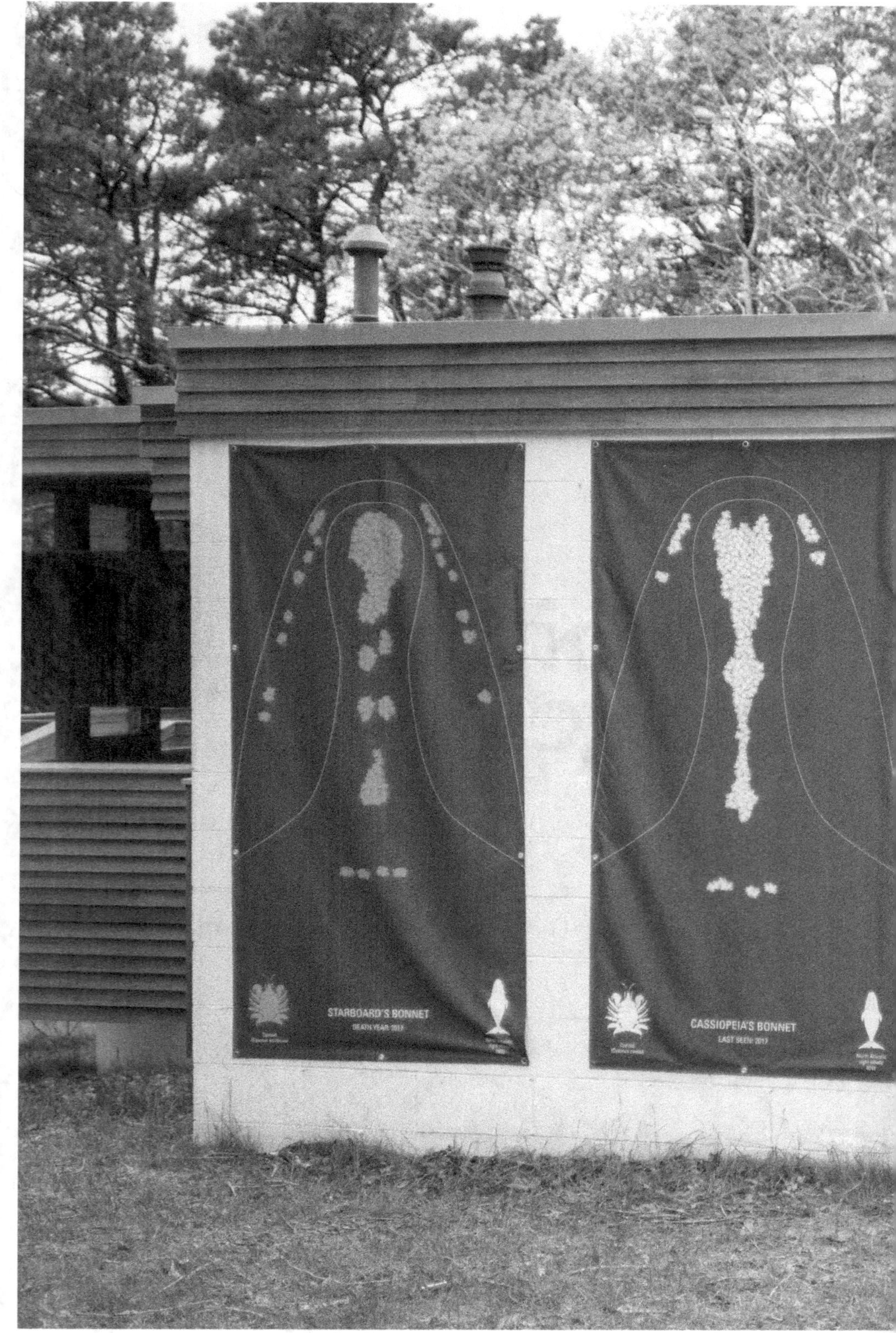

STARBOARD'S BONNET
DEATH YEAR: 2017
CASSIOPEIA'S BONNET
LAST SEEN: 2017

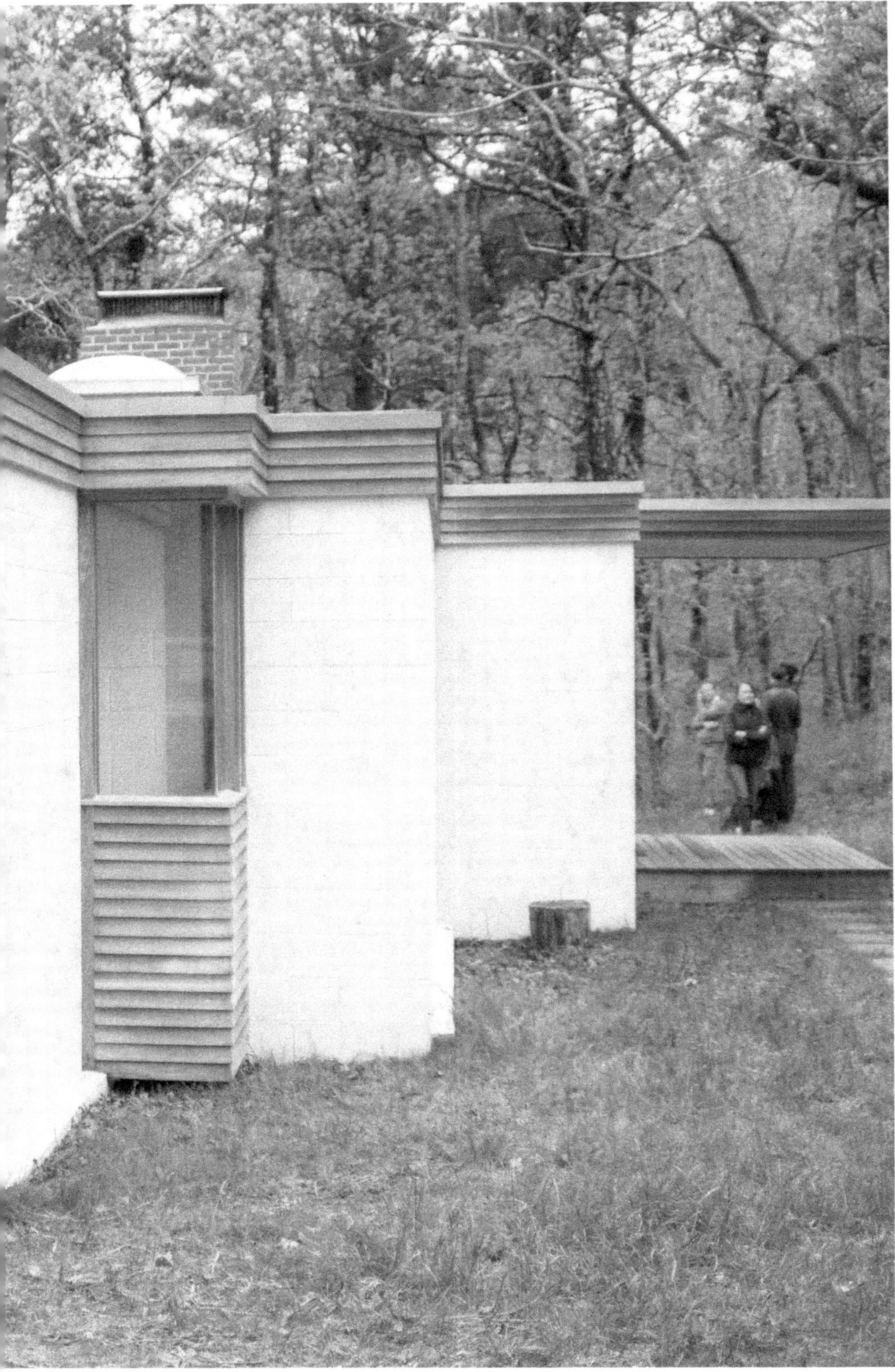

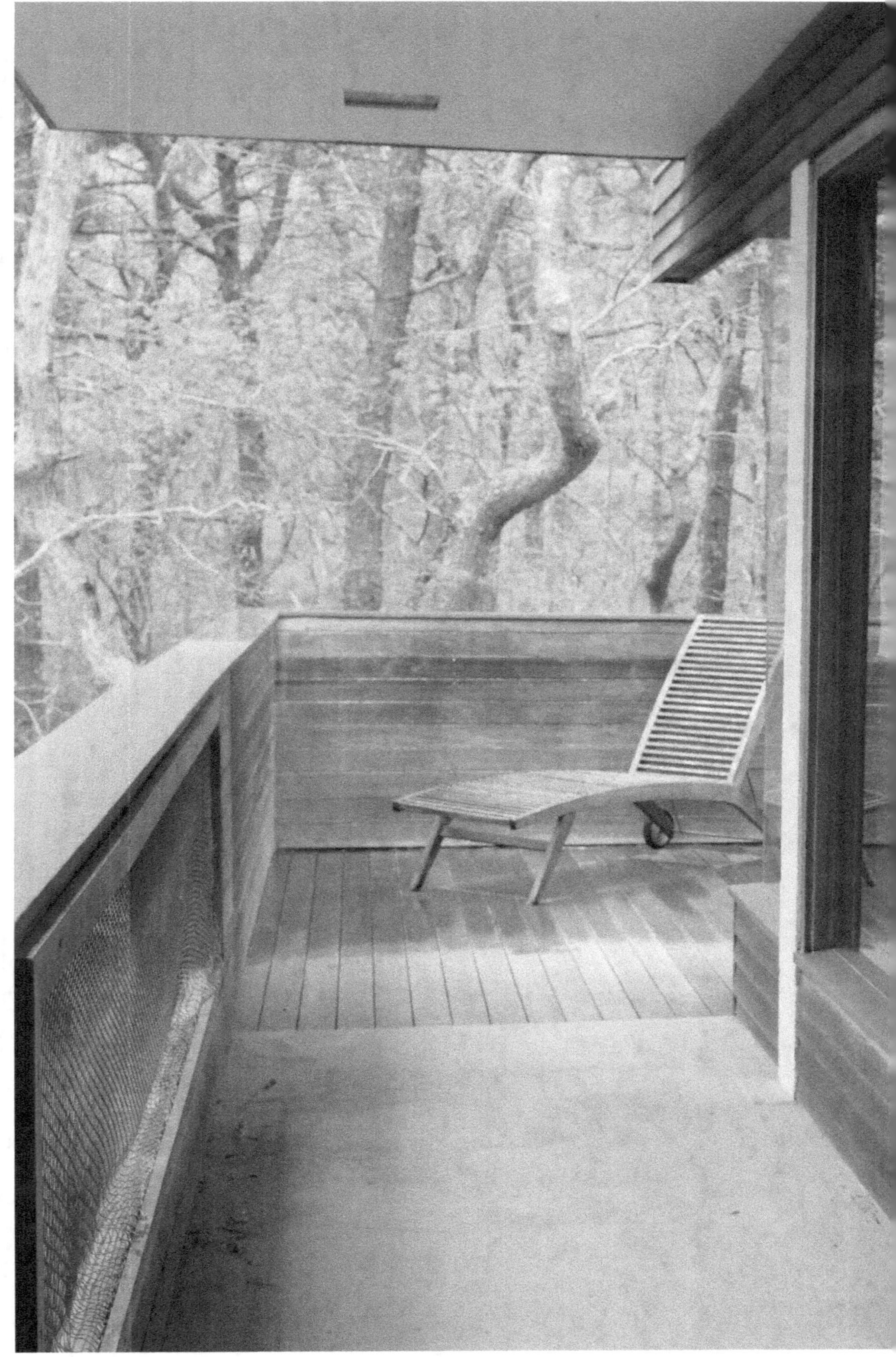

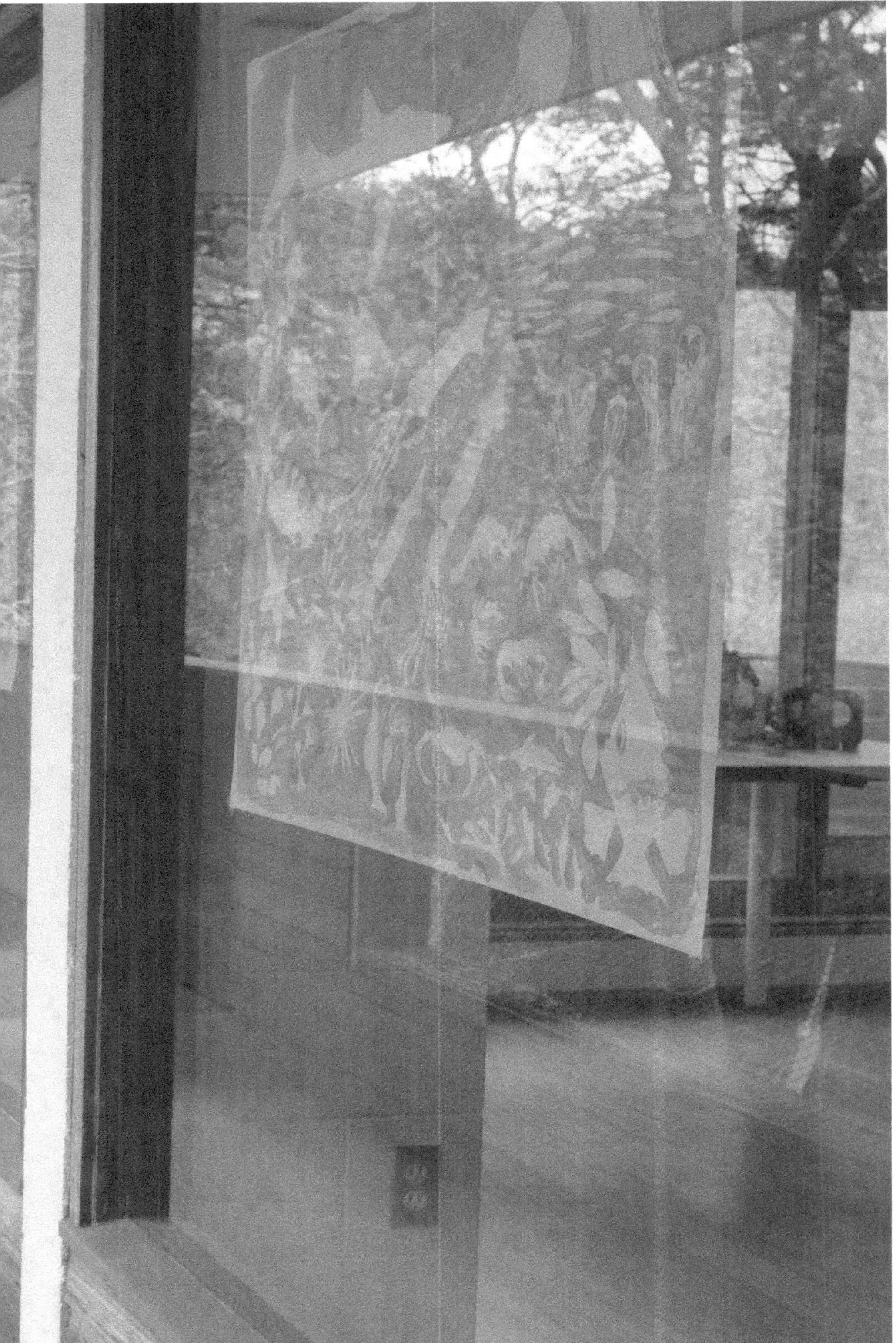

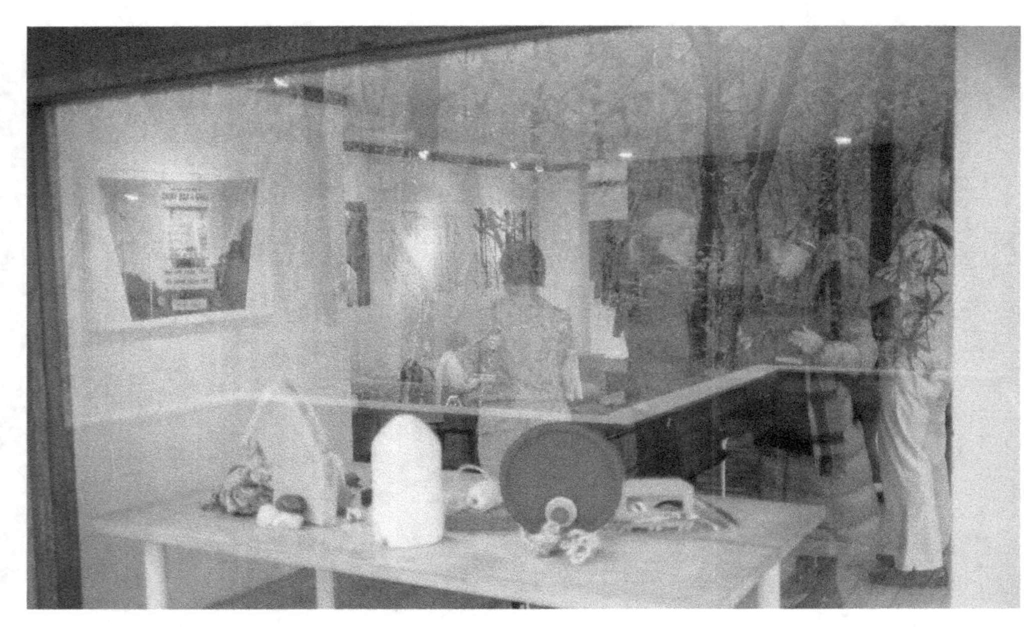

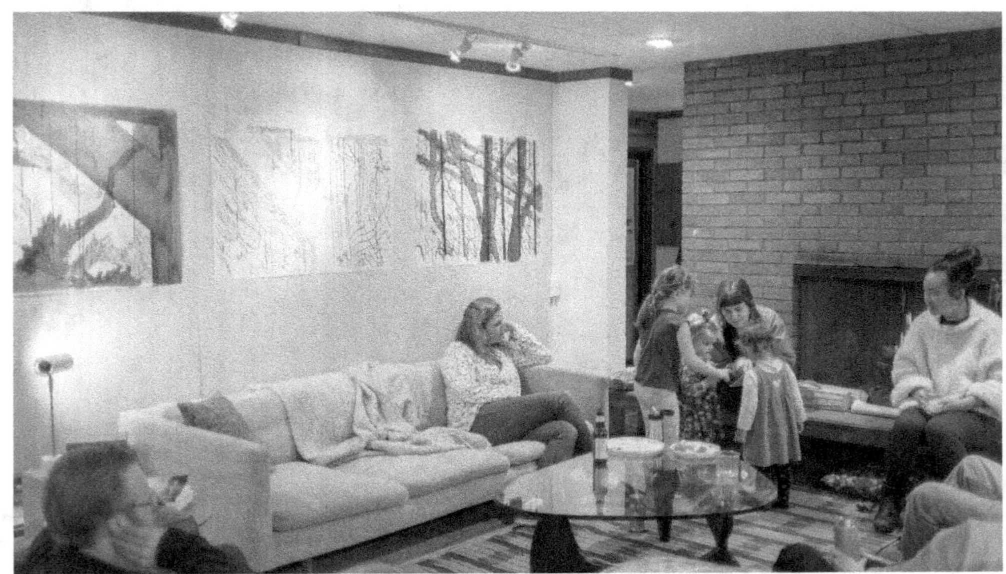

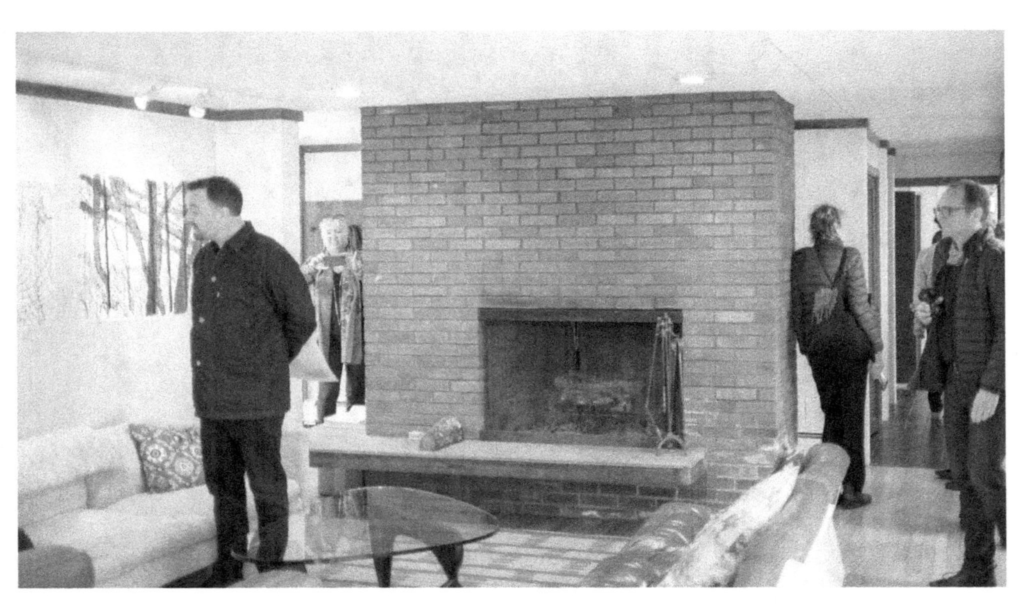

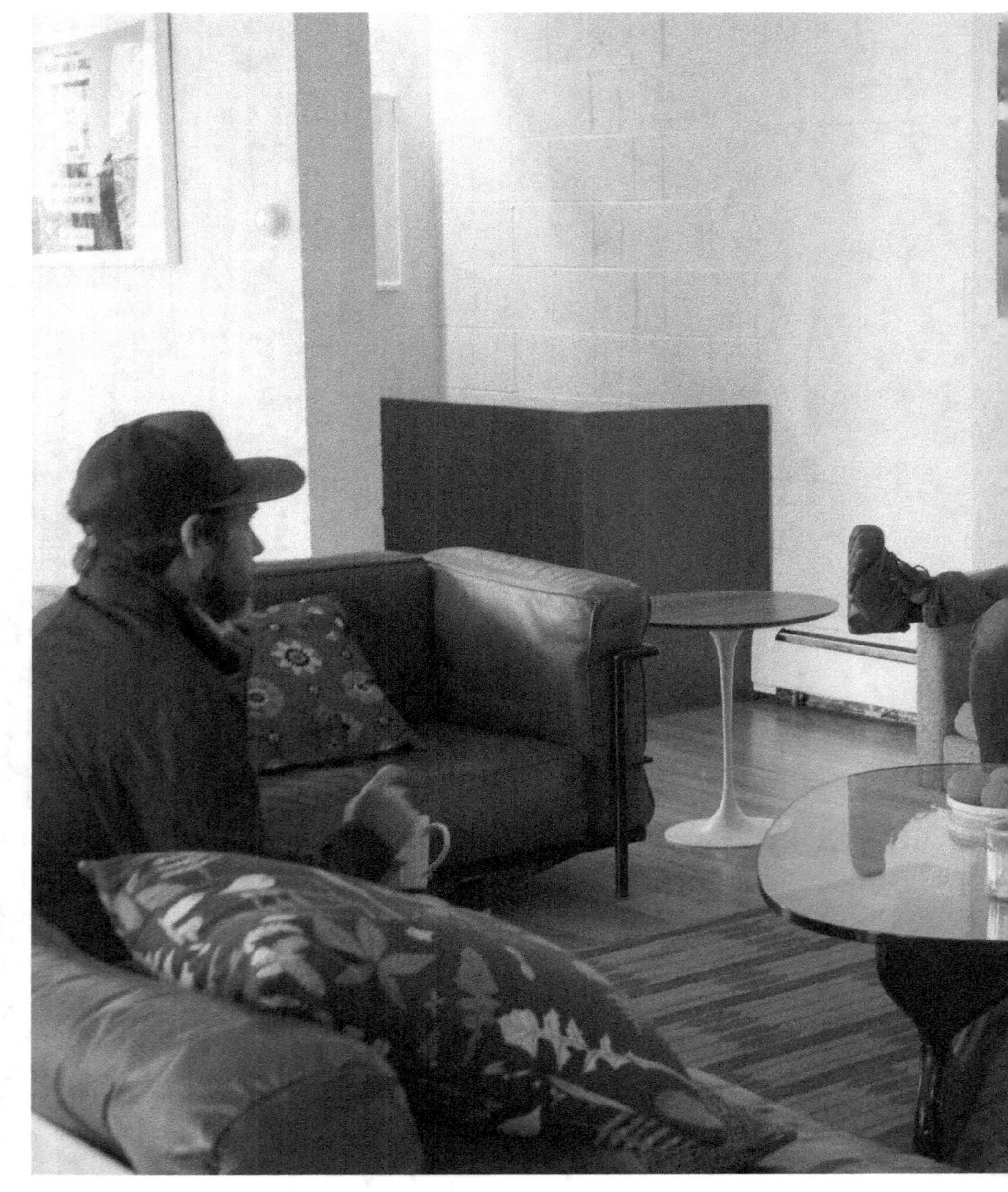

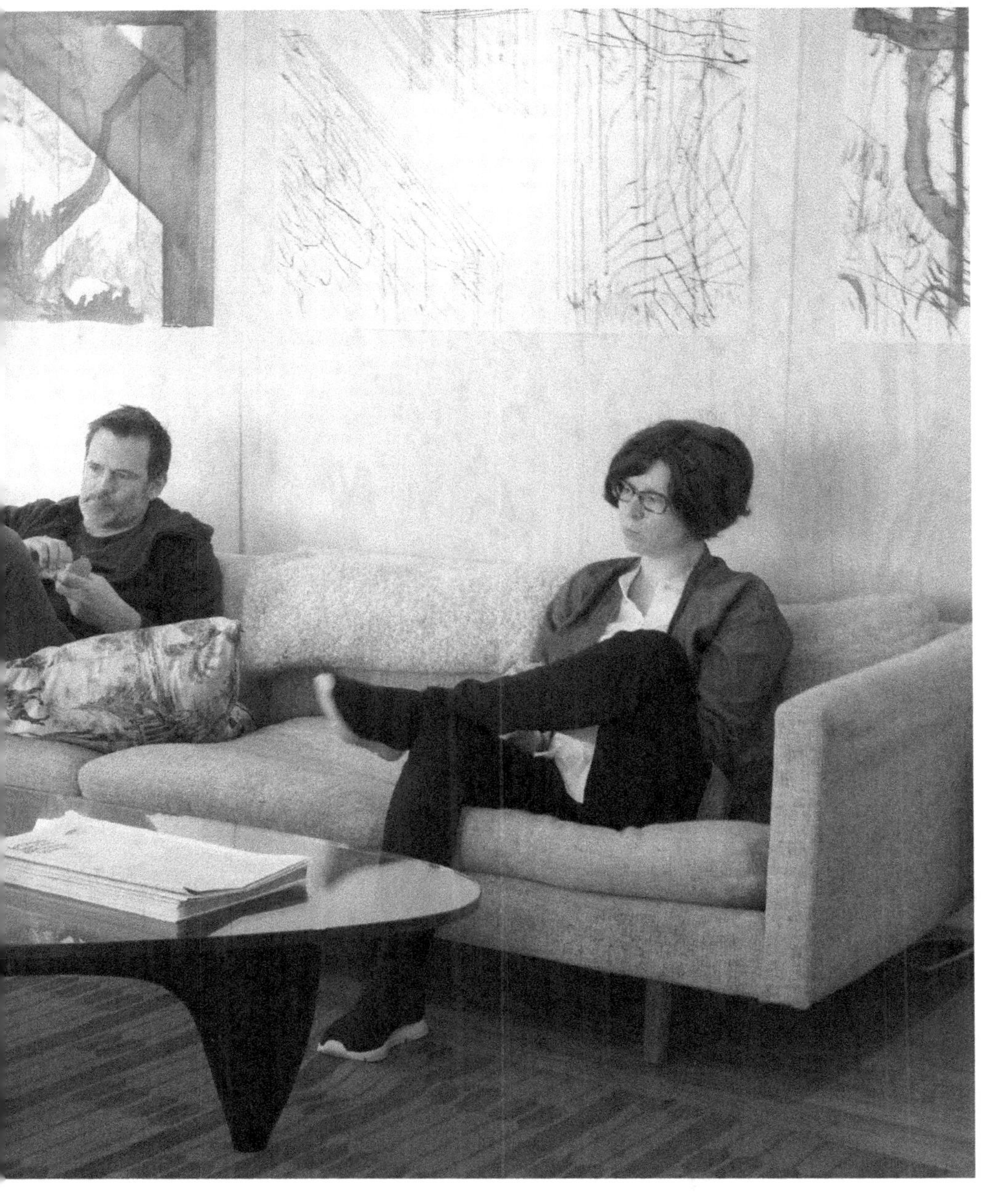

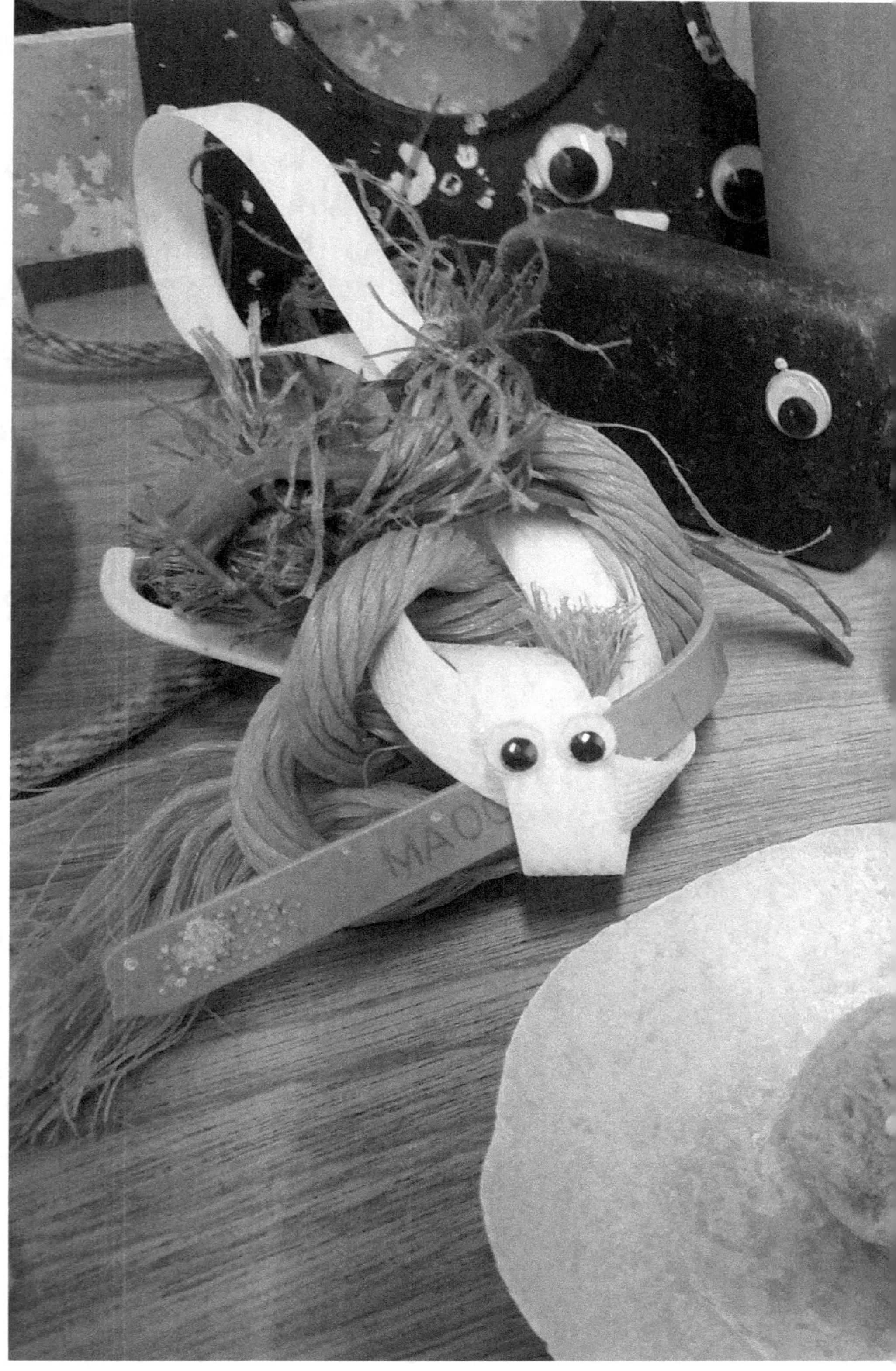

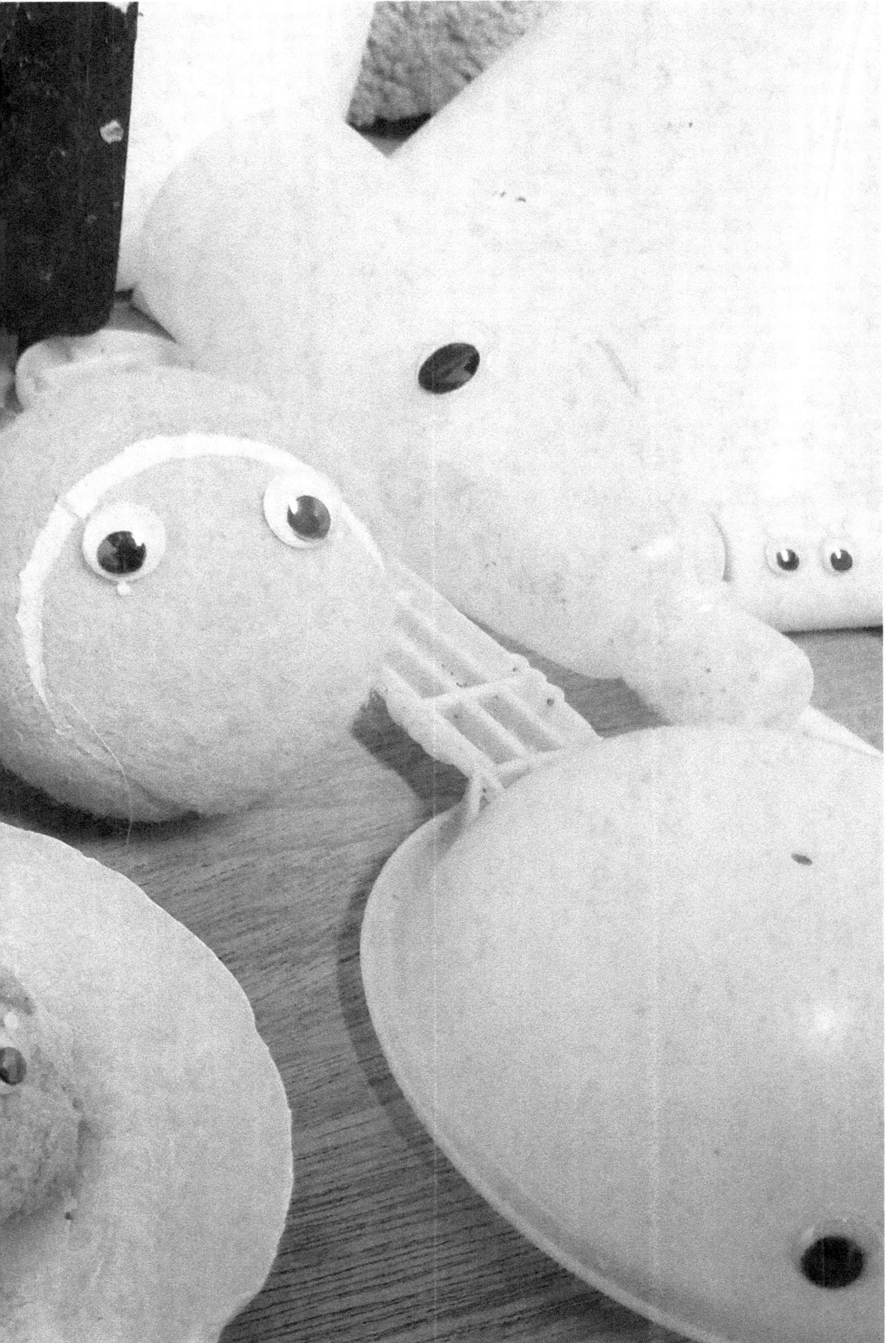

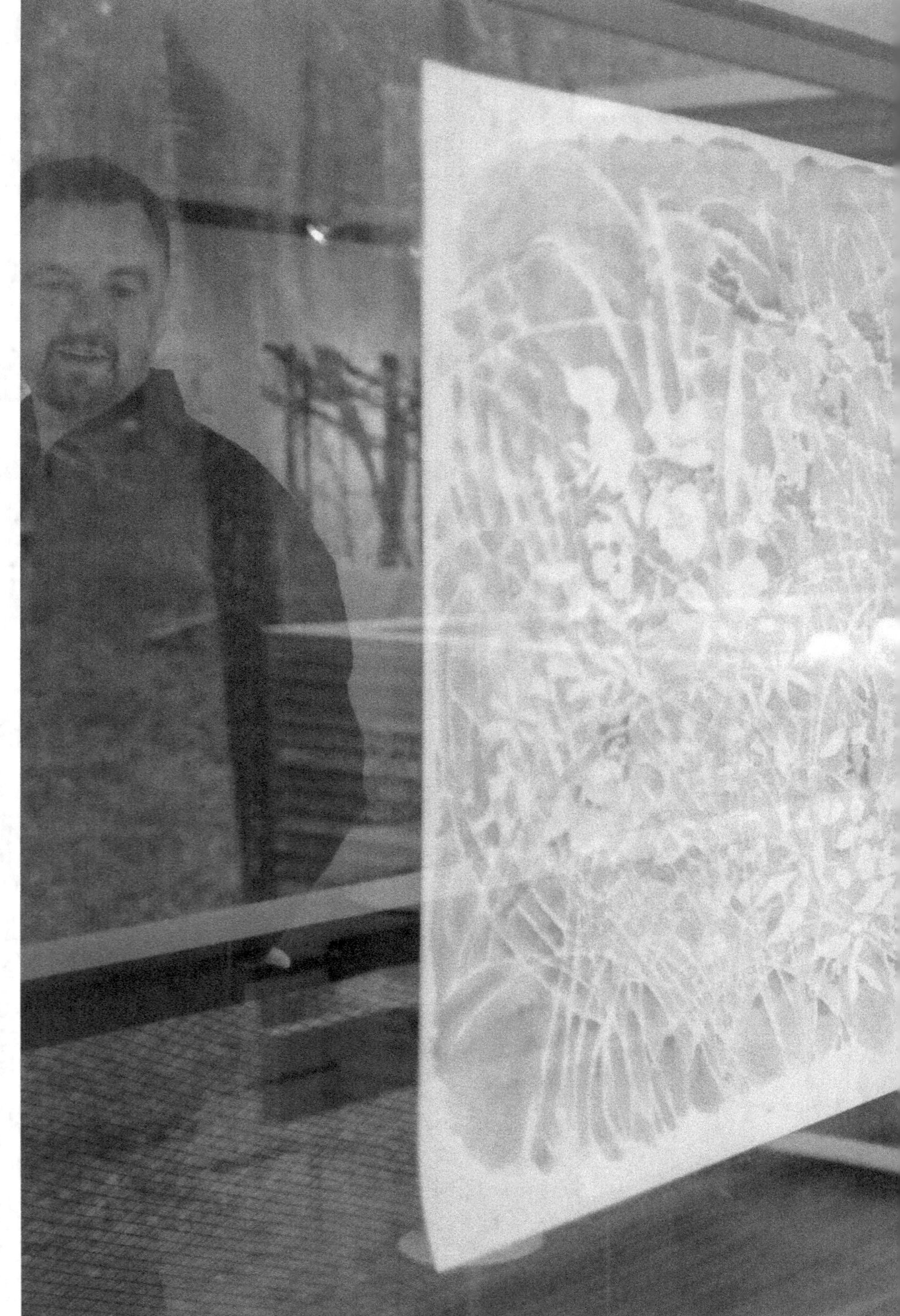

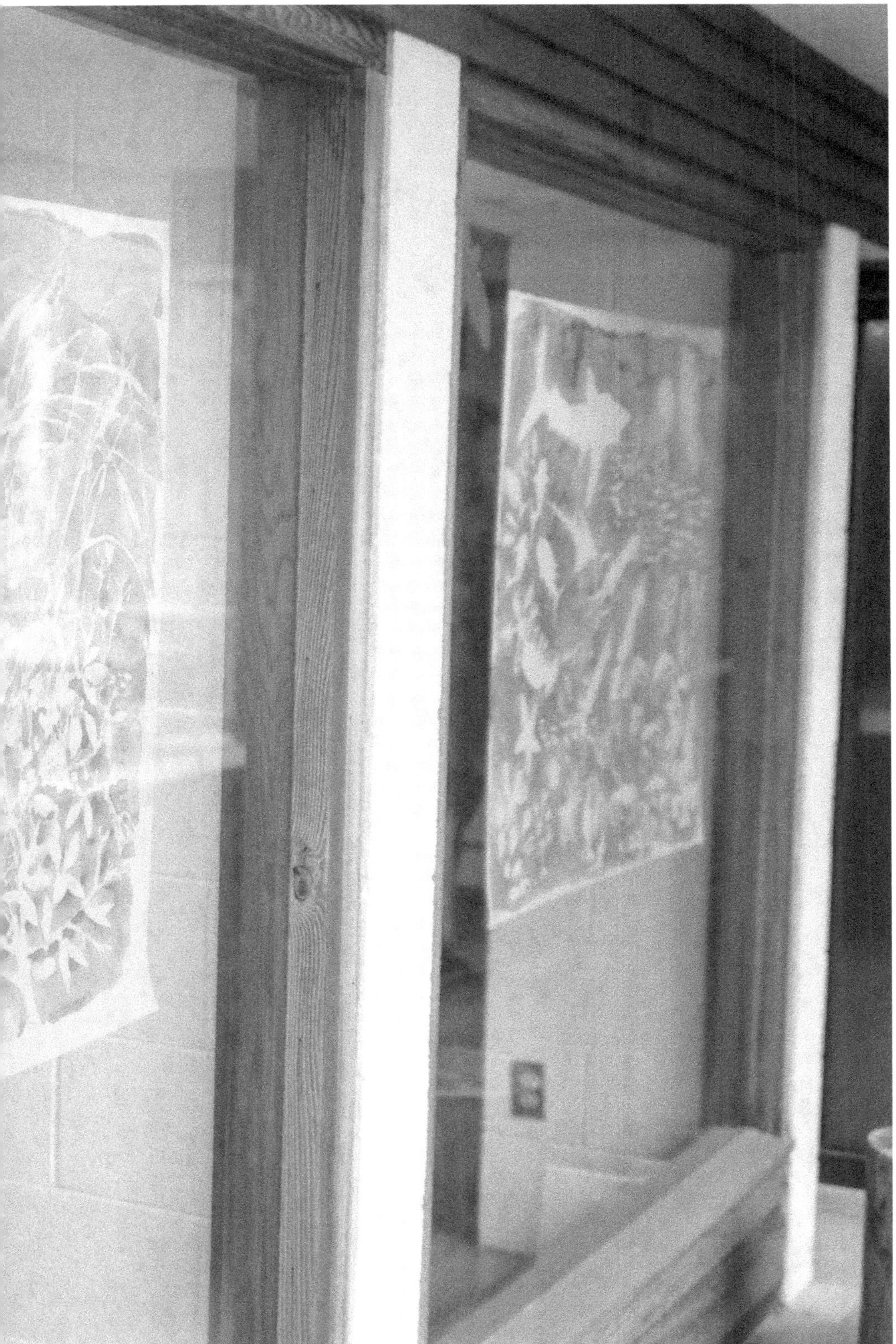

Field Notes

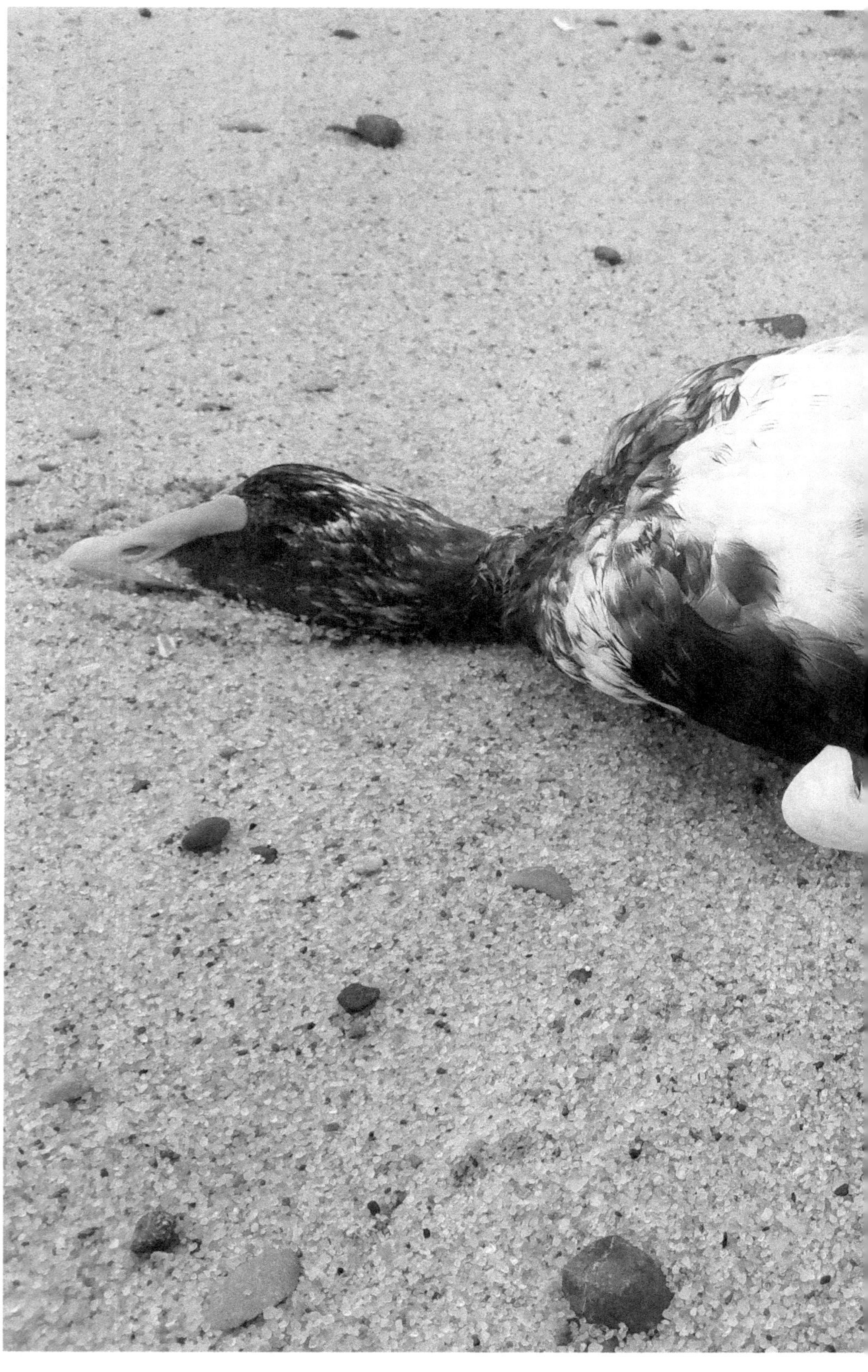

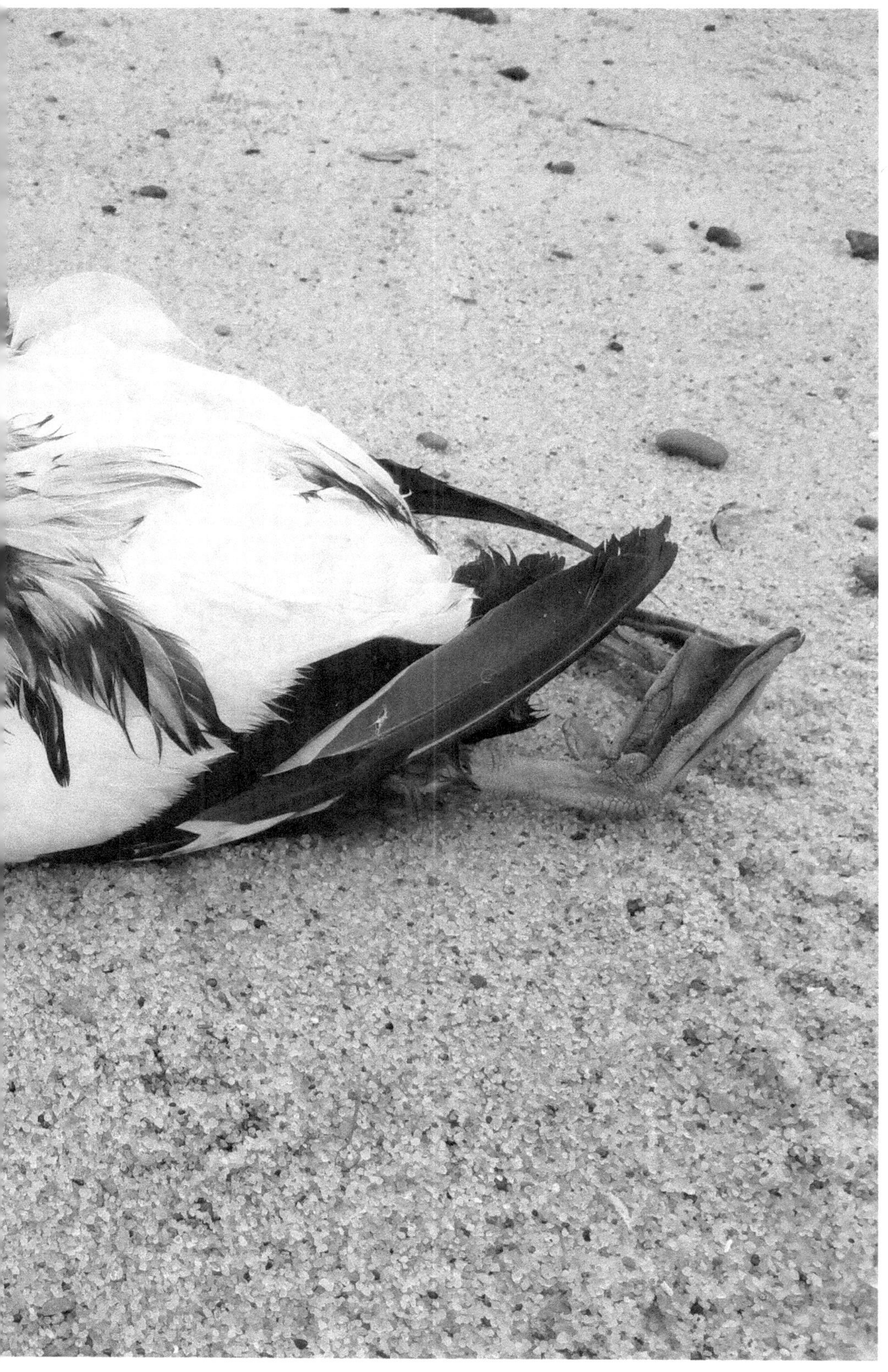

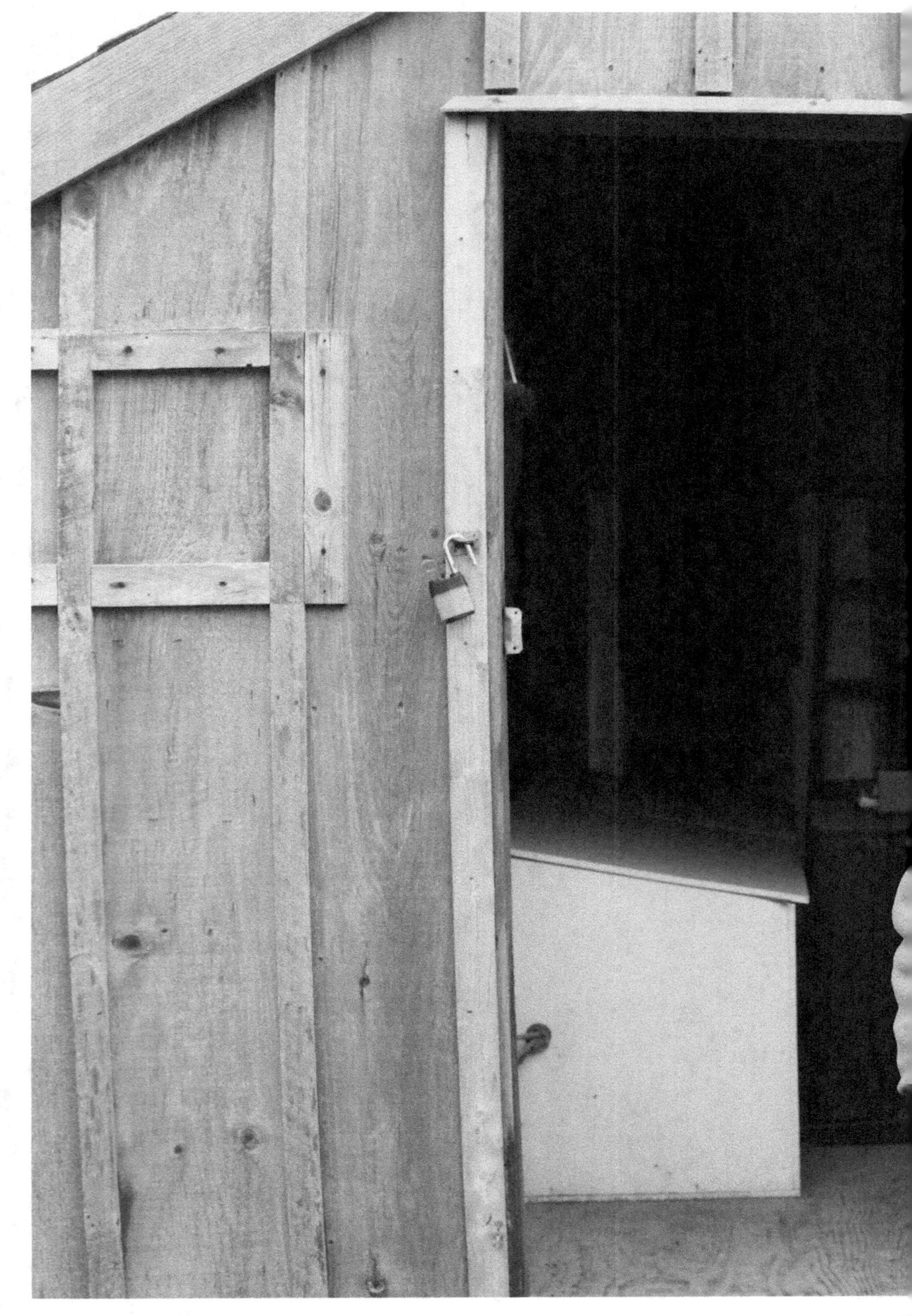

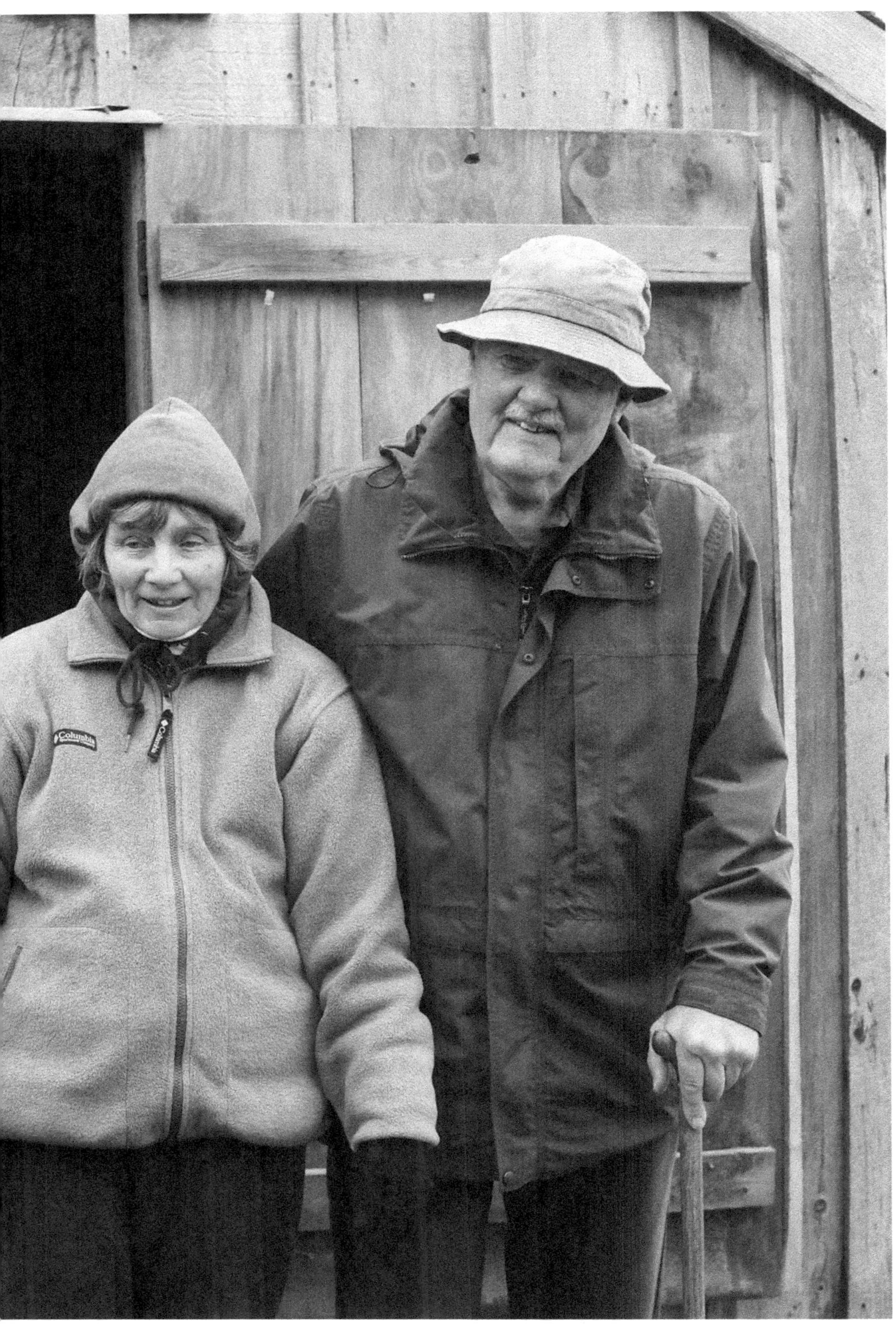

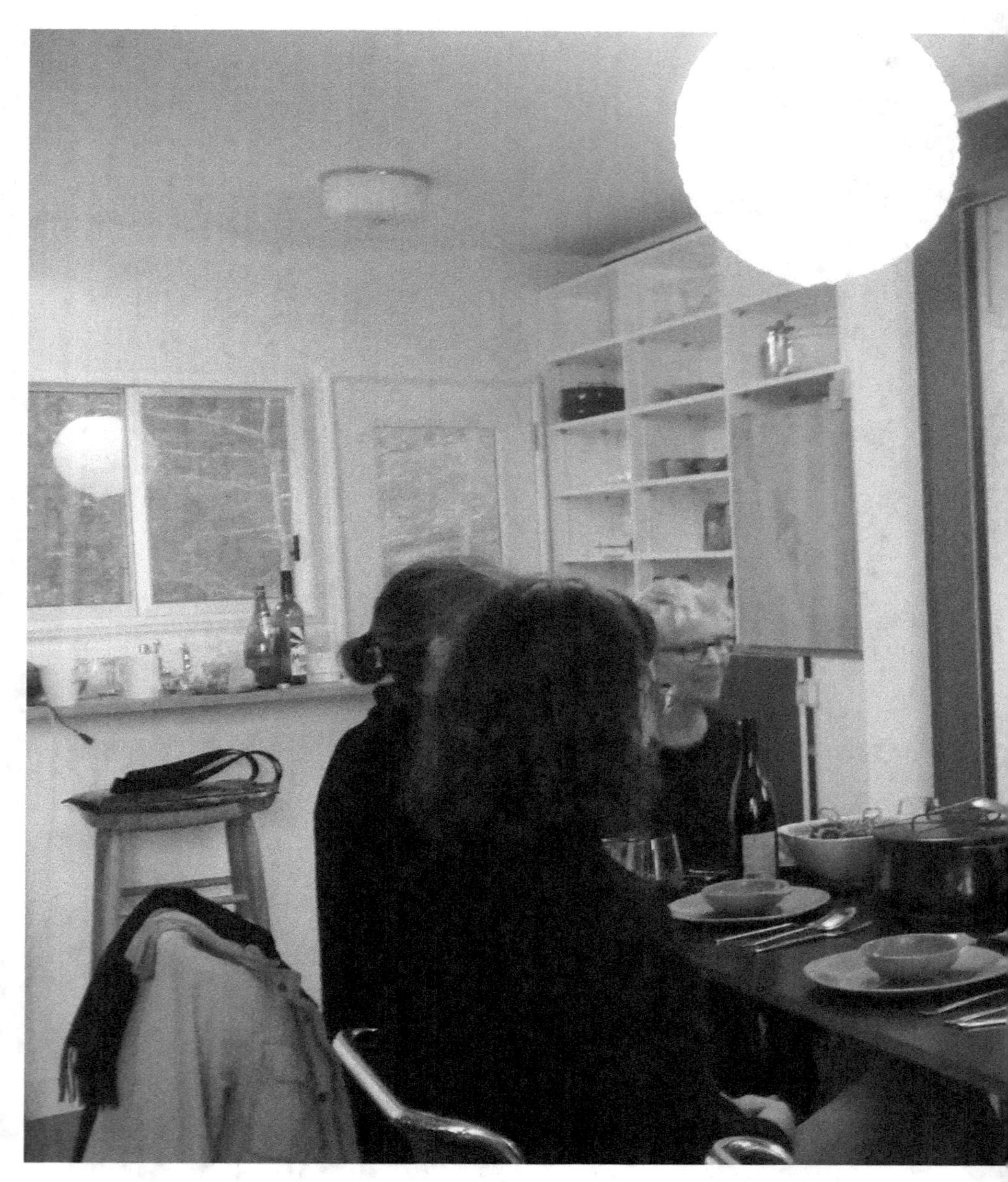

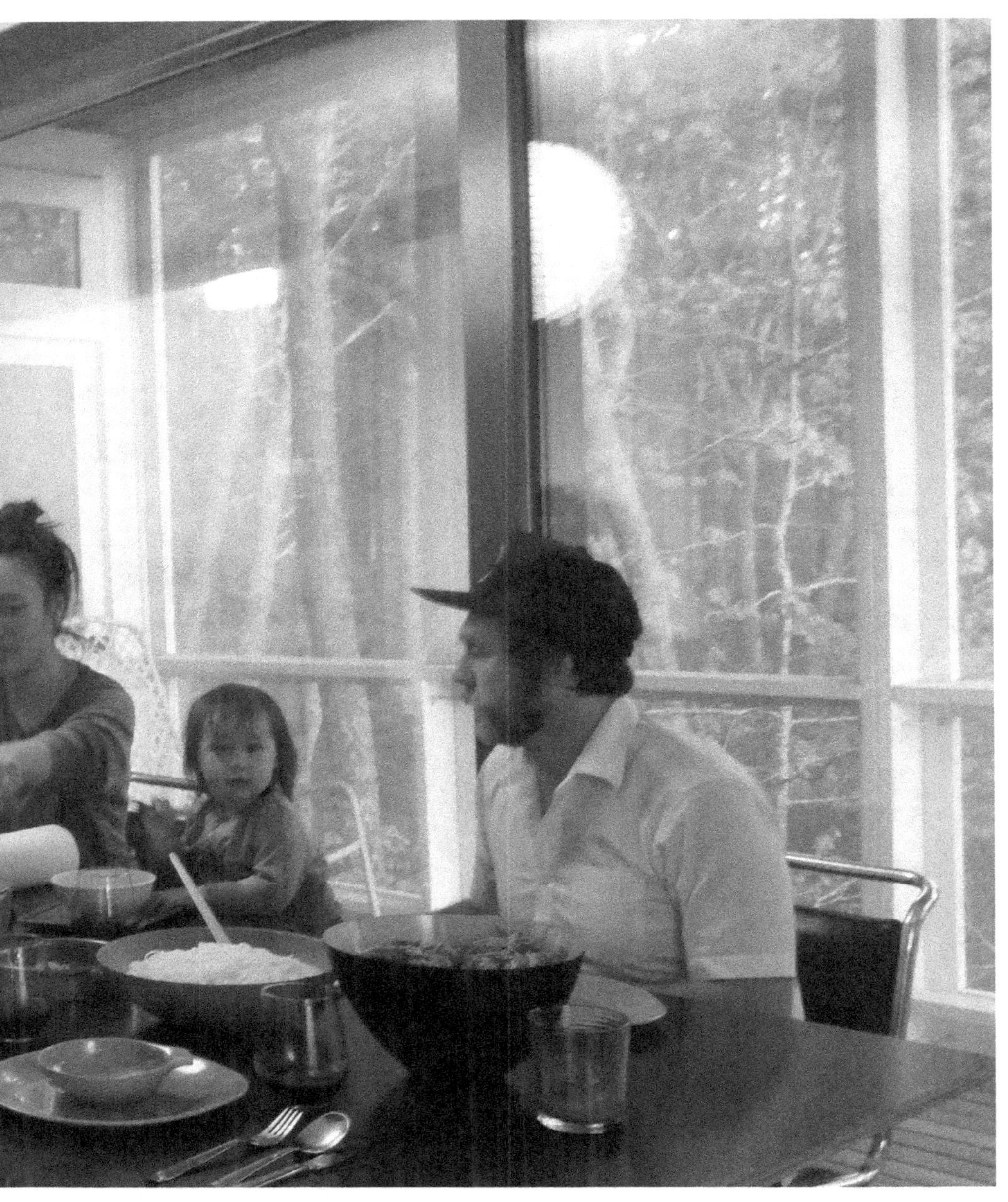

Dinner at Weidlinger house with residents
and Jamie Kruse and Elizabeth Ellsworth from
Smudge Studio.

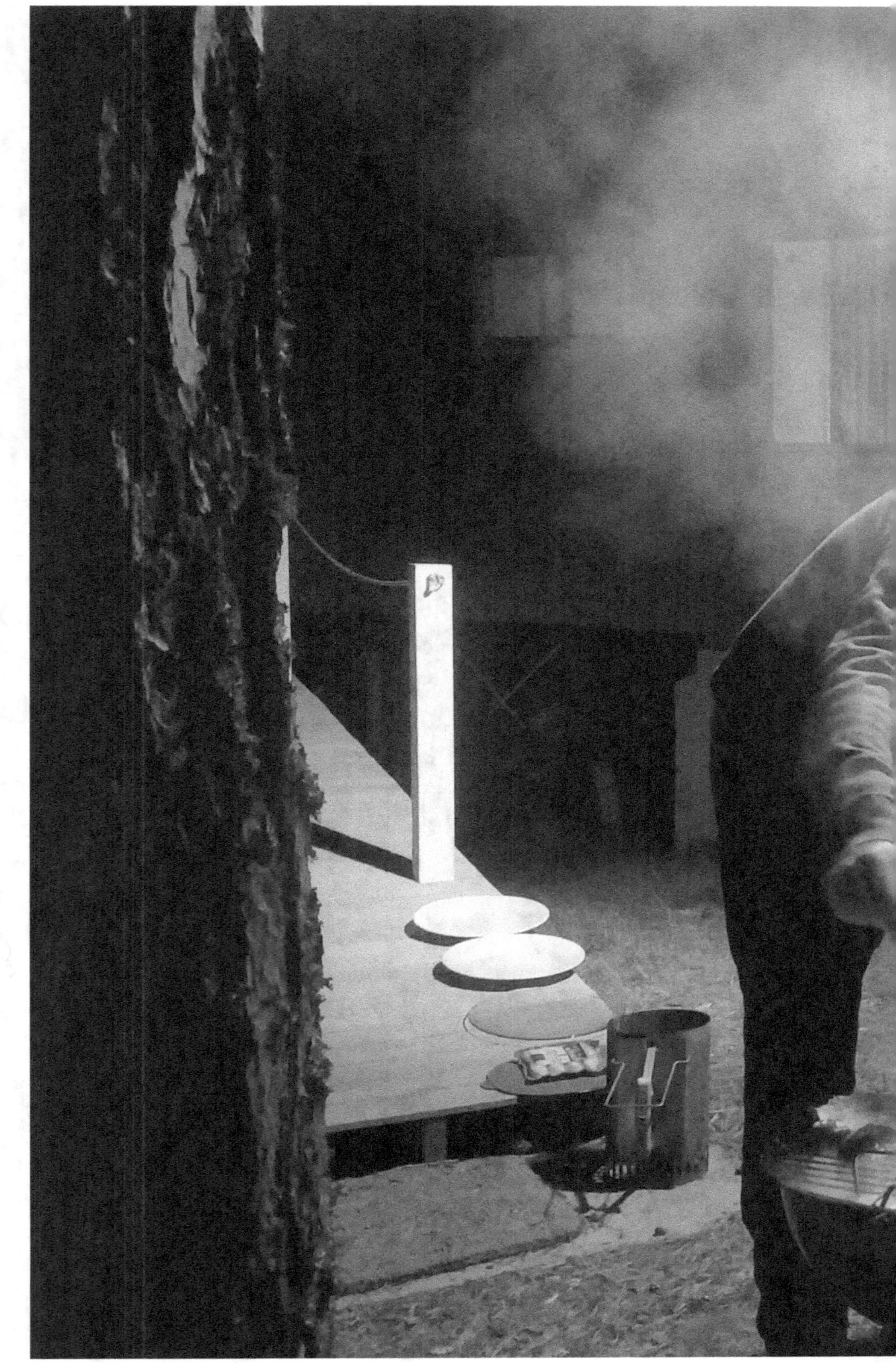

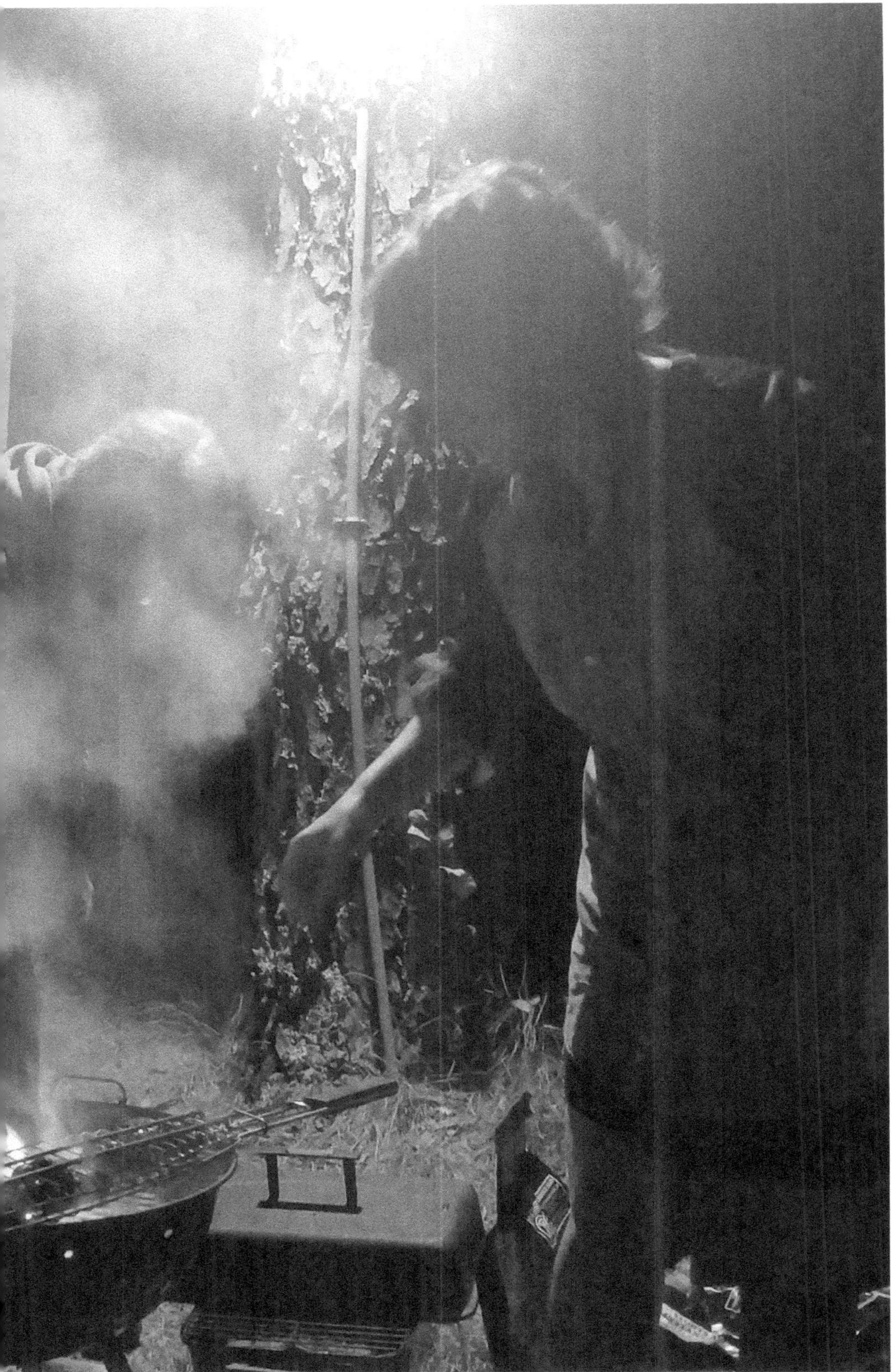

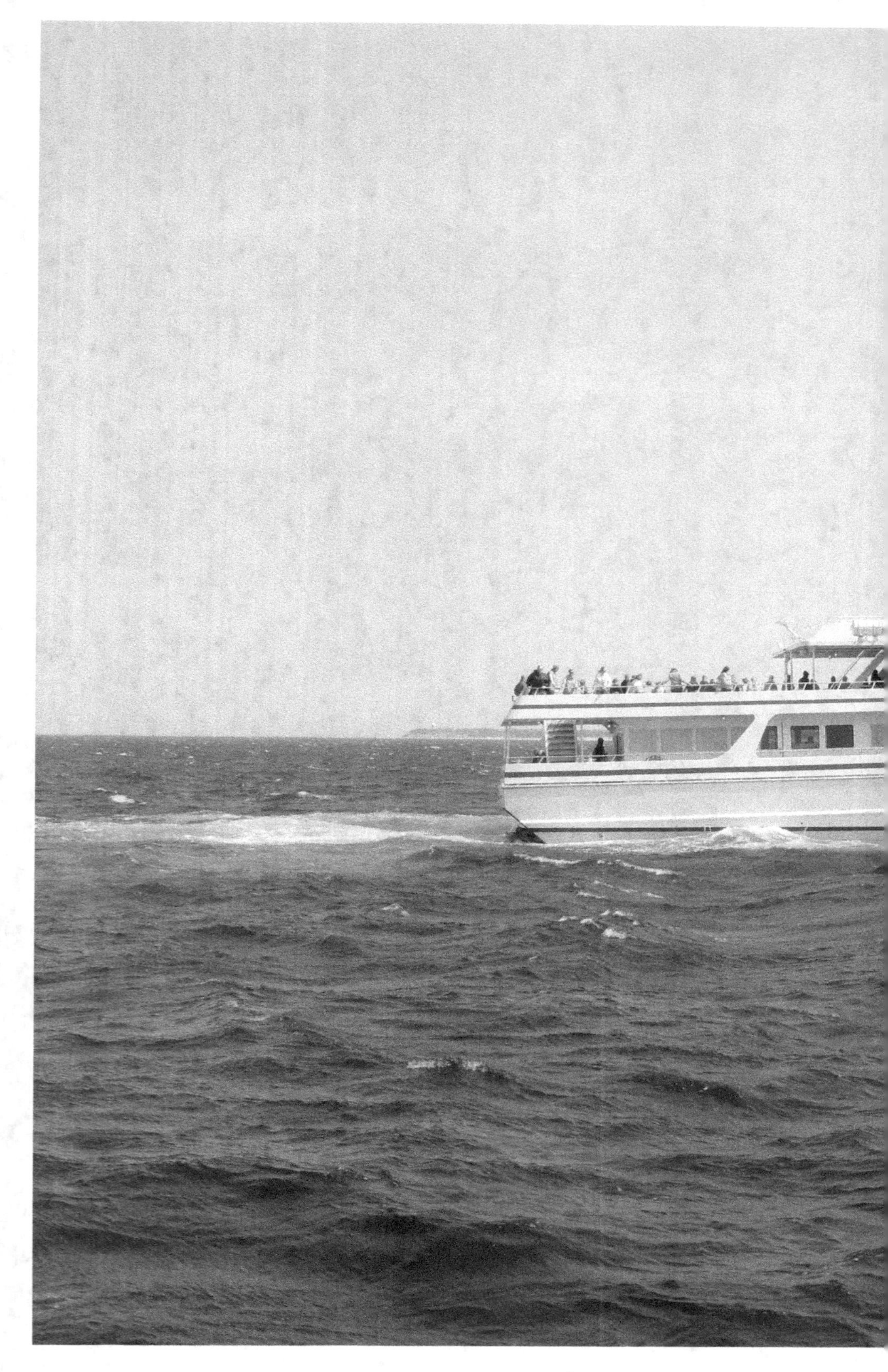

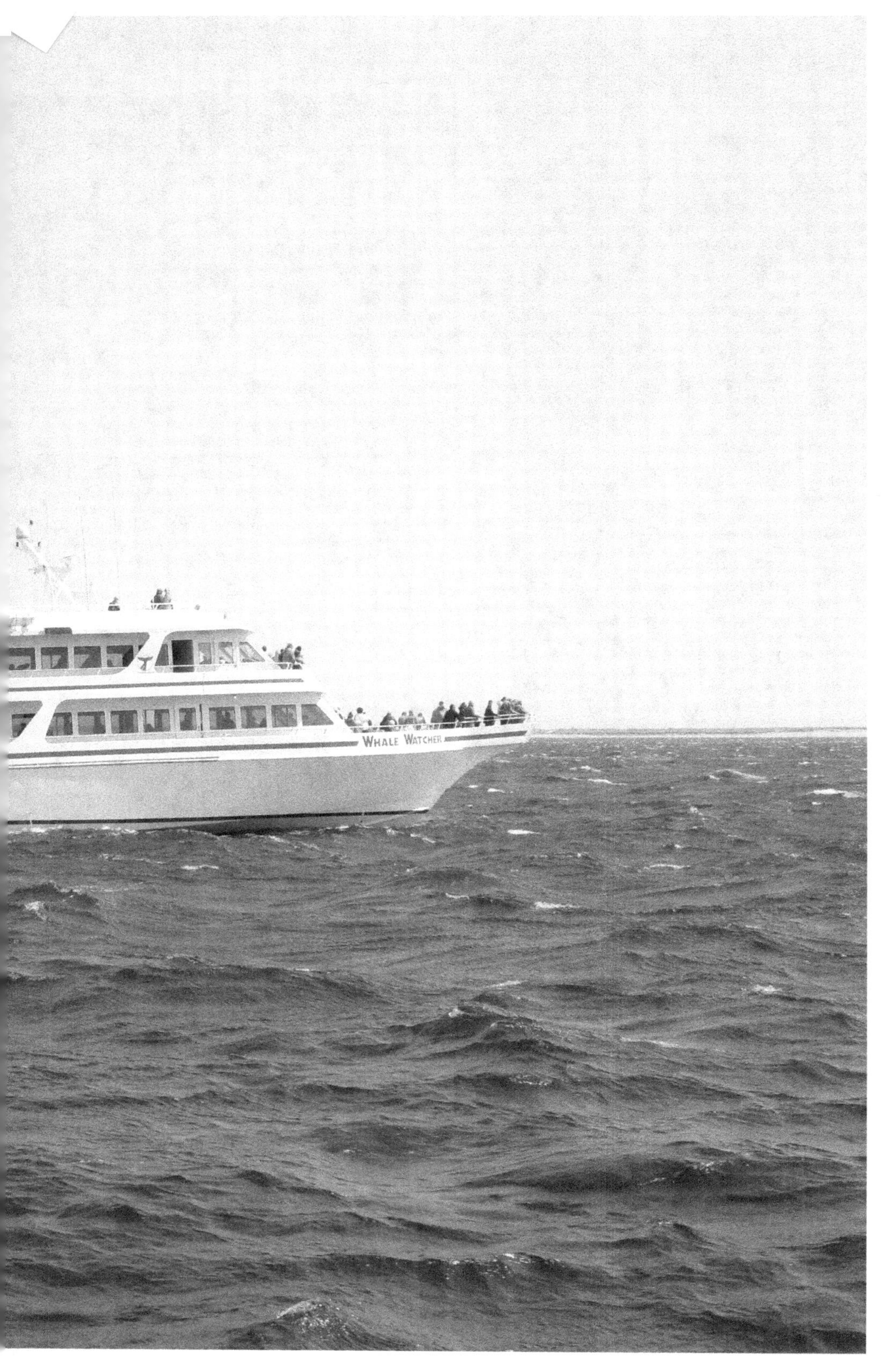
WHALE WATCHER

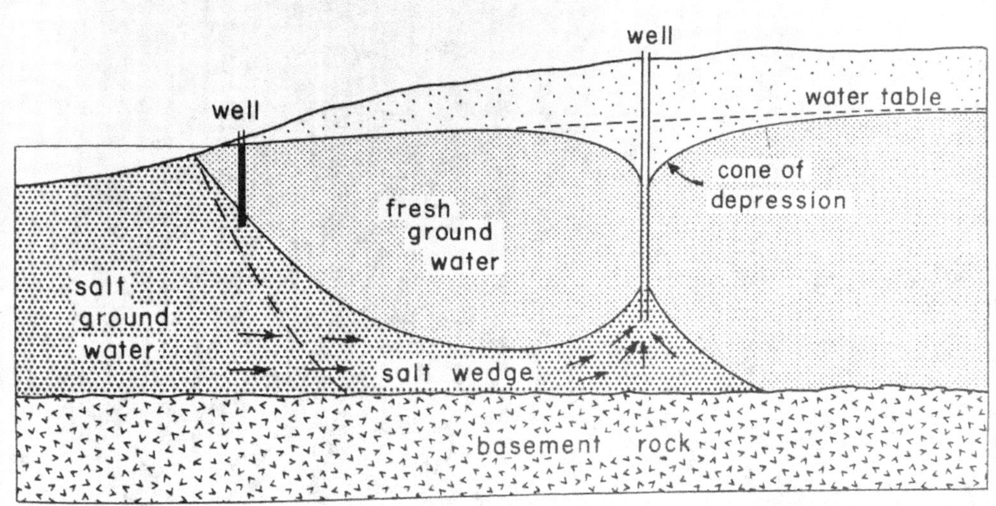

A salt-water wedge beneath the fresh-water zone,
contaminating a large supply well and a small well
near the shore.

Figure 14

Proposed Regime to Govern Interactions Between Marine Mammals and Commercial Fishing Operations

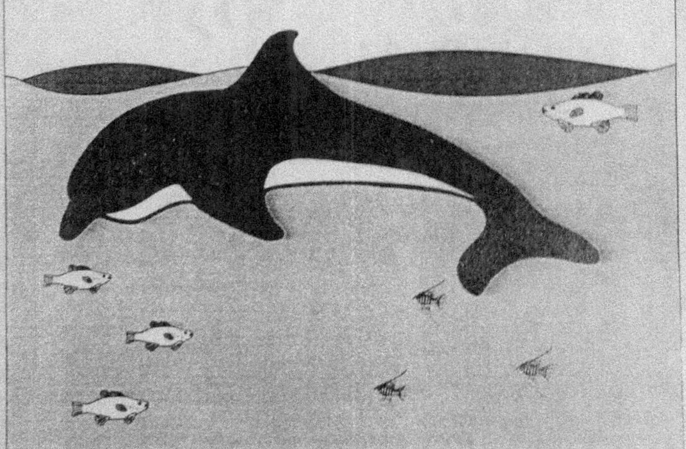

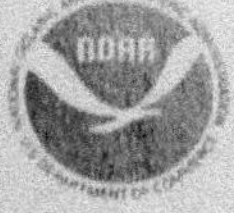

Prepared by

National Marine Fisheries Service
National Oceanic and Atmospheric Administration
U.S. Department of Commerce

November 1992

May 1988

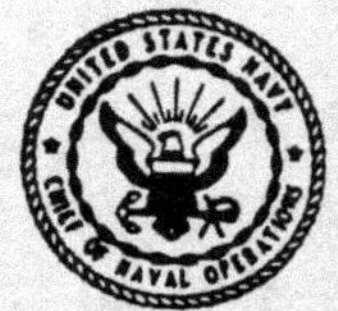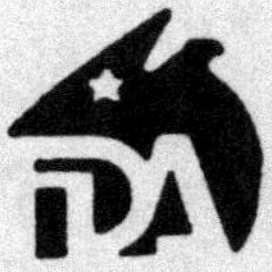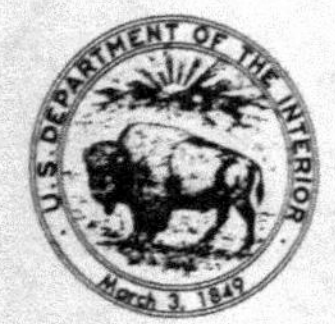

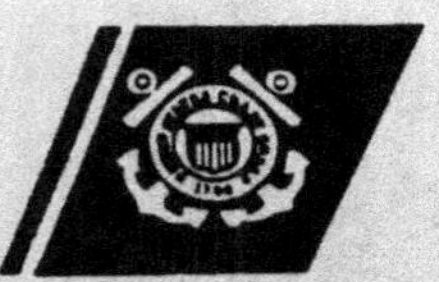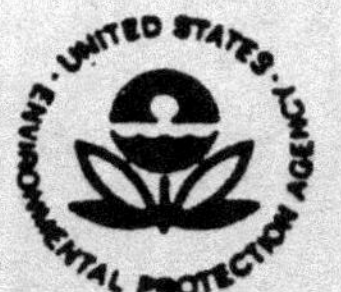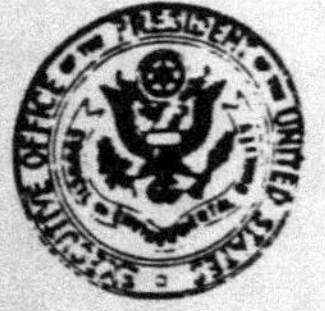

OFFICE OF
DOMESTIC
POLICY

MARINE
MAMMAL
COMMISSION

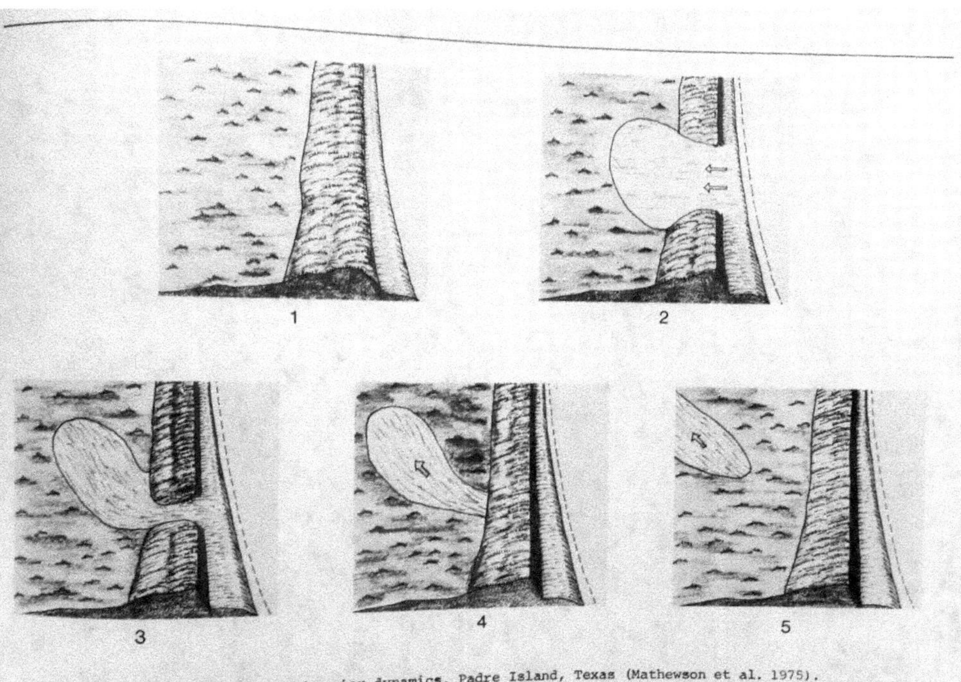

Fig. 77. Model of barrier dynamics, Padre Island, Texas (Mathewson et al. 1975).

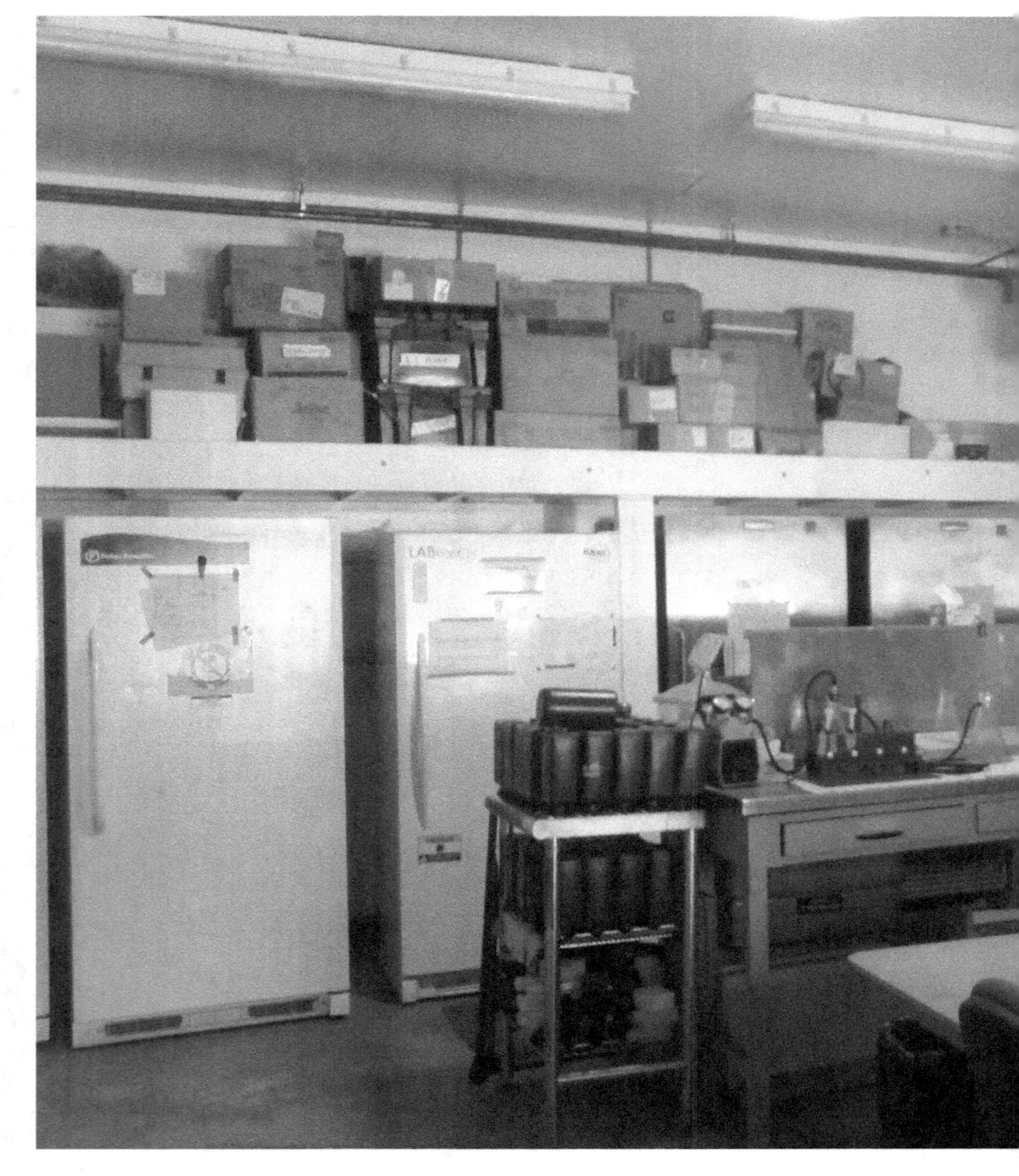

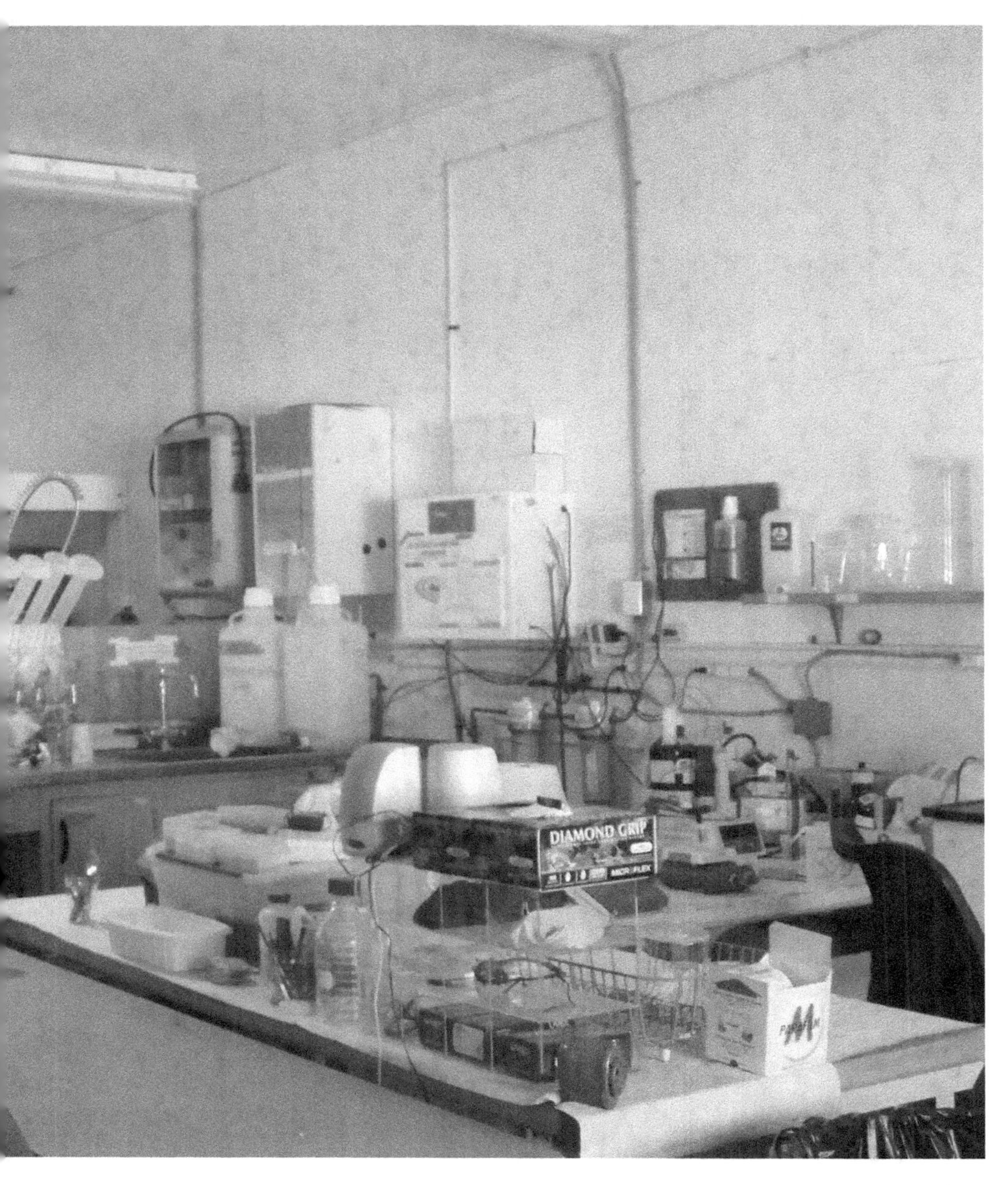

The Lab in Truro

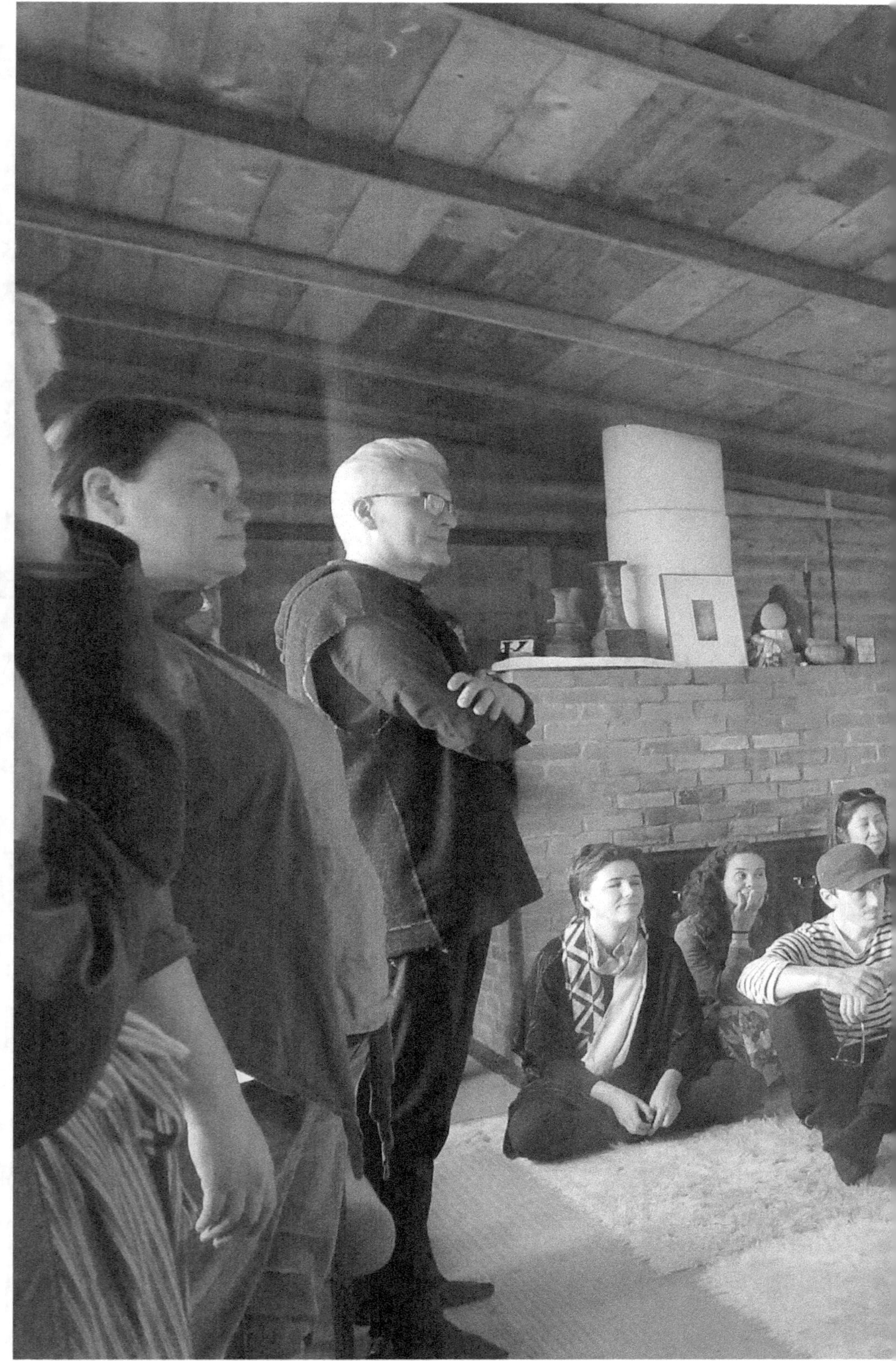

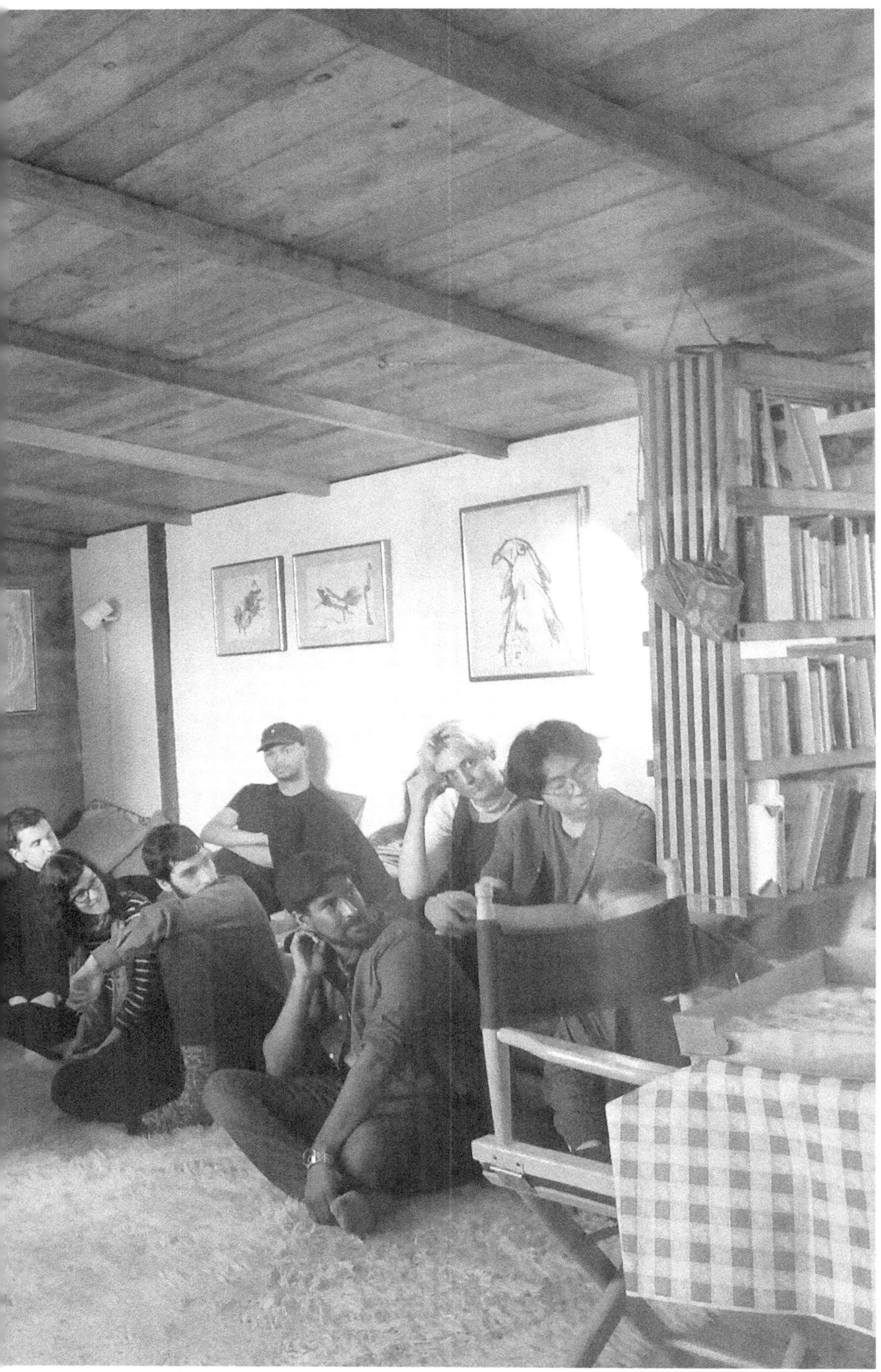

> "Outermost cliff and solitary dune, the
> plain of ocean and the far, bright rims of
> the world, meadow land and marsh and
> ancient moor: this is ... the outer Cape."
>
> —Henry Beston*

Cape Cod...
A Vanishing Scene

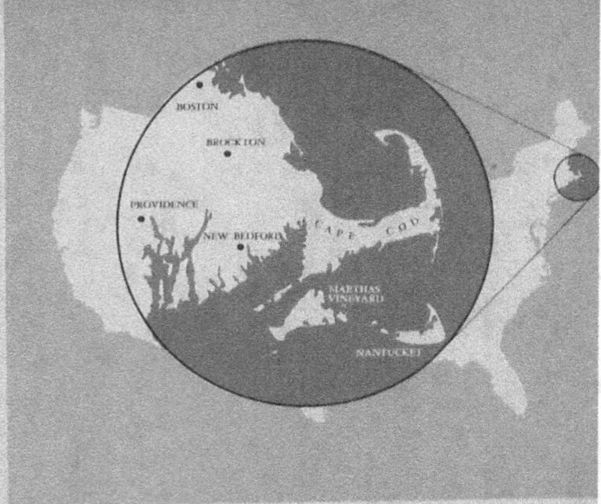

A GREAT PENINSULA, shaped like a bold bent arm, thrusts some seventy miles into the Atlantic Ocean from the Massachusetts mainland. This is Cape Cod, landmark and haven for mariners who sought a new world or wrested their living from a perilous sea. Here vacationists now seek refreshment along sweeping shores and quiet coves.

Heaped up by glaciers long ago; then molded by winds and waves and currents, Cape Cod has been endowed with plant and animal life in rich variety. Now it is a scene of everchanging charm, beautiful to behold, fascinating to study. Surf pounds the eastern headland. Calmer waters of Cape Cod Bay and Nantucket Sound wash the Cape's northern and southern shores. Between, the winds brush heath and marsh and woodland, ruffling ponds the glaciers left behind.

On the ocean side of the Cape's forearm lies Great Beach, a magnificent ocean shore. For three centuries, this extraordinary shoreline was spared the great industrial buildup of our eastern

*HEADLANDS mark Great Beach, "the outermost of outer shores."**

Aerial photograph by Kelsey

Front Cover: Silvery beach grasses cling to the dunes around Pilgrim Lake, North Truro.

Photograph by Samuel Chamberlain

* from *The Outermost House*, Rinehart & Company, publishers.

Participant Bios

Mark Adams is a painter, printmaker, and cartographer who has worked for the National Park Service on Cape Cod since 1991. He lives in North Truro where his favorite mapping tools are his running shoes. He studied ecology, landscape architecture, and scientific illustration at the University of California, Berkeley, and drawing at California College of the Arts. He has worked as a gymnastics coach, forest firefighter, and fish taxonomist. A recent retrospective was called "Expedition" at the Provincetown Art Association Museum (September–October 2017). He is represented by the Schoolhouse Gallery in Provincetown.

Jean Barberis is a maker, an artist, and a curator, but he rarely makes a distinction between the various aspects of his practice. His work almost exclusively revolves around collective initiatives. A native of Provence, Barberis co-founded Flux Factory and is currently the Artistic Director. Barberis is more engaged as an artist in the curatorial process and the ability to foster collaborations while encouraging the production of ambitious new works. His interests are vast and varied and include urban exploration, shoemaking, boat building, and engaging in exchanges and economies outside of the confines of capitalism.

Joshua Edwards is the author of several books of poetry. Born on Galveston Island, he lives with his family in Chicago and West Texas, where he directs a small press, Canarium Books, and works at bookstores.

Brooklyn-based artist **Marie Lorenz** has been exploring and documenting urban waterfronts for many years. In 2005 she started her Tide and Current Taxi, taking participants through New York City using only the tide. Each trip is planned to coincide with strong tidal currents in the New York harbor, all documented with pictures and stories at tideandcurrenttaxi.org.

Nancy Nowacek is a Brooklyn-based artist, designer, and educator. Her interests are based in urban design, movement, and communication. She makes art engaged with power and politics of the body in late-capitalist, post-industrial culture. Her work intervenes into the designed world via sculpture, performance, and installations that challenge and shift assumptions of the social and body schema. Nowacek was a 2018 summer fellow at Socrates Sculpture Park, and has previously been supported by a fellowship at Eyebeam, and residencies through the Lower Manhattan Cultural Council, Recess, Signal Fire, and the Sharpe Walentas Studio Program. She teaches at the Stevens Institute of Technology, and organizes exhibitions, panels, and events devoted to waterways and climate change as well as bodies and technology. She has presented works in New York, Los Angeles and the Bay Area, Canada, South America, and Europe.

Kendra Sullivan & Dylan Gauthier are a Brooklyn-based artist duo focused on deep research, eco-poetics, collaboration, public engagement, and the built environment. They co-founded SUNVIEW LUNCHEONETTE, a space for art, politics, and action in Greenpoint, Brooklyn in 2012, and are members of the eco-art collective *Mare Liberum*. Gauthier holds an MFA from Hunter College, and is faculty at Parsons/The New School. Sullivan is Director of the Seminar on Public Engagement and Collaborative Research at the CUNY Graduate Center, and is a PhD candidate in English (Environmental Humanities) with an MA in Sustainability and Environmental Education.

Jeff Williams was born in Cambridge, MA in 1976. He now splits his time between Austin, TX and Brooklyn, NY. Williams has been awarded several fellowships and residencies including The American Academy in Rome, The Core Program, Headlands, and most recently at the Recycled Artist In Residency. Solo exhibitions of Williams work include the Jack Hanley Gallery, 1708 Gallery, the Contemporary Austin, and Artpace. Group exhibitions include Museum of Contemporary Art Detroit, Regina Rex, Canada, Socrates Sculpture Park, Museum of Fine Arts Houston, and Lora Reynolds Gallery

Lynn Xu was born in Shanghai. She is the author of *Debts & Lessons*, which was a finalist for the LA Times Poetry Prize, and the chapbook, June. She lives with her family in Marfa, TX, and Chicago, IL, where she teaches at the University of Chicago.

Marina Zurkow is a media artist focused on near-impossible nature and culture intersections. She uses life science, materials, and technologies – including food, software, animation, clay, and other biomaterials – to foster intimate connections between people and non-human agents. Recent solo exhibitions of her work include bitforms gallery in New York; Chronus Art Center, Shanghai; the Montclair Art Museum, New Jersey; Diverseworks, Houston; her work has also been featured at FACT, Liverpool; San Francisco Museum of Modern Art; Walker Art Center, Minneapolis; Smithsonian American Art Museum, Washington D.C.; Museum of Fine Arts, Houston; Wave Hill, New York; Borusan Collection, Istanbul; 01SJ Biennial, San Jose; Brooklyn Academy of Music; Museum of the Moving Image, New York; Creative Time, New York; The Kitchen, New York; Ars Electronica, Linz, Austria; Transmediale, Berlin; Eyebeam, New York; Sundance Film Festival, Utah; Rotterdam Film Festival, The Netherlands; and the Seoul Media City Biennial, Korea, among others. Zurkow is a John Simon Guggenheim Memorial Fellow. She has also been granted awards from the New York Foundation for the Arts, New York State Council for the Arts, the Rockefeller Foundation, and Creative Capital. She is represented by bitforms gallery.

First published in 2020 by punctum books, Earth, Milky Way.

https://punctumbooks.com

ISBN-13: 978-1-950192-94-6 (print)

ISBN-13: 978-1-950192-95-3 (ePDF)

DOI: 10.21983/P3.0325.1.00

LCCN: 2020940935

Library of Congress Cataloging Data is available from the Library of Congress

Book design: Partner&Partners — partnerandpartners.com

Cover image: Dylan Gauthier, 2018

~ with much gratitude to Eileen A. Joy and Vincent W.J. van Gerven Oei at punctum books.

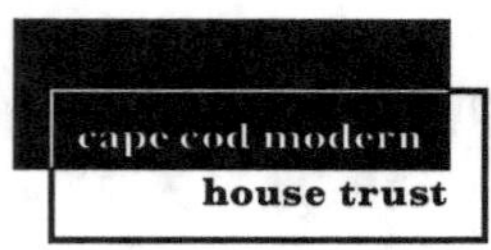

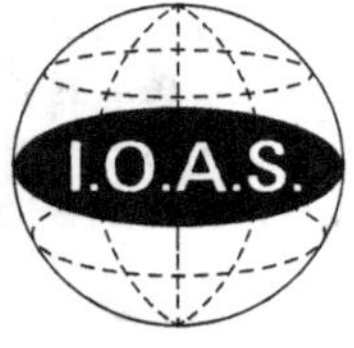

Institute for Ocean
Art and Science